Open Learning
in
Early Childhood

Open Learning
in
Early Childhood

Barbara Day

University of North Carolina, Chapel Hill

Macmillan Publishing Co., Inc.
New York
Collier Macmillan Publishers
London

Acknowledgments

Special recognition and many thanks to

1. The teachers and administrative staffs of the Frank Porter Graham Child Development Center, University of North Carolina, Chapel Hill, and the Jeffreys Grove School, Wake County School System, Raleigh, North Carolina, for their cooperation and support in allowing most of the photographs in this book to be taken in their classrooms and learning centers.

2. Graduate students in early childhood education at the University of North Carolina, Chapel Hill, for their enthusiasm, ideas, and interest in this publication.

Copyright © 1975, Barbara Day
Printed in the United States of America

Macmillan Publishing Co., Inc.
866 Third Avenue, New York, New York 10022

Collier–Macmillan Canada, Ltd.

Library of Congress Cataloging in Publication Data

Day, Barbara, (date)
  Open learning in early childhood.

  Bibliography: p.
  Includes index.
  1. Open plan schools. I. Title.
LB1029.06D38   372.1'3   74–5717
ISBN 0-02-327950-8

Printing: 2 3 4 5 6 7 8   Year: 5 6 7 8 9 0

CONTENTS

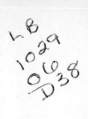
To Our Godchildren—
Billy, Beth, Dave, Andrew,
Vince, John, Rachel, and Barbara—
who share with us the joys of early childhood

INTRODUCTION

Open Learning in Early Childhood is designed to help early childhood teachers, administrators, and supervisors provide an open education learning environment for young children. Such an environment is child–centered and invites independent and group learning through explorationaand investigation. It is carefully planned with varied and challenging materials so that each child is able to create and discover the many joys that learning has to offer.

In a learning environment with children ranging in chronological age from five to eight, and whose actual developmental span is far greater, a tremendous amount of diversified materials is necessary in order to meet individual needs, interests, and abilities. The environment must be one that provides for all areas of development, including the specific social, emotional, motor, and cognitive requirements of early childhood. Such an environment is based on the following beliefs:

1. Children grow and develop at different rates and that rate is separate and distinct from that of any other child. This rate of development is often unrelated to chronological age.
2. Children are naturally curious and eager to learn, and they learn best when they are able to follow many of their own interests and desires to learn.
3. Learning is something a child does, rather than something done to him.
4. Play is a child's way of working and learning.
5. Children learn from each other; they learn to experience a sense of responsibility and achievement, to respect themselves and others, and to learn how to learn.
6. A rich learning environment, one deliberately designed with much to explore and to discover, is essential in helping young children learn basic skills. Concrete and sensory materials are a vital part of this environment, as they are basic learning devices for the young child.
7. Basic skill development is considered essential in an open education learning environment; however, a variety of creative approaches to teaching and learning, including an integrated day, is suggested.
8. The development of initiative and self-reliance is encouraged in an atmosphere of trust and structured freedom.
9. Each child is a unique individual and must be appreciated and valued for his individuality in all areas.

An early childhood learning environment should be a comfortable, colorful place where children and adults can live together in a happy and relaxed atmosphere. This environment can be designed with large complexes or open-spaced schools where teachers work together in teams, or it may be designed for self-contained open classrooms. Physical structure does not determine openness; however, it may facilitate the process. The inside area should be large and carpeted, if possible, with many windows and easy access to the outside, which is a vital part of the total learning environment.

Learning centers or areas provide the core of an early childhood open environment, and this volume discusses ten such centers. Each learning center is organized into the following categories: environmental resources, materials (commercial and teacher-made), objectives, and suggested activities. The suggestions in each center include a sampling of activities appropriate to the particular area and are not intended to be inclusive of all activities found in each center. Basic textbooks and other resource materials will continue to be a part of the total program.

The possibilities for centers are limitless. When appropriate, they should contain self-correcting activities at various levels of difficulty which require a minimum of teacher direction. An attractive center will invite investigation and provide opportunities for the involved child to learn through exploration that which he is ready to learn. Centers may be prepared by the teacher with a specific objective in mind, or perhaps be an eclectic arrangement of interesting items where the child finds his own purpose, or they may be assembled spontaneously to meet a particular interest of the moment.

An important element of an open environment is its "openness." Activities flow from one area to another and every possibility for optimal use of space is explored. There may, of course, be physical limitations depending on the design of the structure, but whenever possible, the flow should include the outdoors, halls, a parent room or space where parents are involved with children, and perhaps the kitchens and cafeterias of the school. Learning centers and areas should be well planned to allow ease of movement and accessibility.

The organization of the learning areas changes with changing needs. The curriculum often evolves rather than always being prescribed. Choice is provided, depending on the needs and interests of each child. Children and adults are open and sensitive to each other.

How might an open early childhood learning environment appear to an observer? Imagine yourself visiting an environment such as this for the first time.

You have heard of an open learning environment such as the one you are about to visit, but somehow you feel it will be different from the verbal descriptions. You finally reach the building and you are impressed by the outdoor learning environment. You notice the flower and vegetable gardens, the play equipment, the animals, and many children of various ages engaged in a number of activities. As you move closer, you see that the outside has different sections (cement patios and grassy areas) with doors leading to the inside from these areas. One child is sitting in a small rocking chair on the grassy area reading *Charlotte's Web*. A small group of children on the patio are "building a city" with blocks. A young boy comes up to you, says "hello," asks your name and hands you a yellow flower. You walk to another area that houses animals. There are fine homemade cages and pens containing chickens, ducks, rabbits, and guinea pigs. The animals are being fed and cared for by enthusiastic children. A seven-year-old girl is instructing a five-year-old boy how to hold a rabbit correctly.

On around the school is a play area with gymnastic equipment, tire swings, slides, climbing poles, etc. You turn your attention briefly to a small red-haired boy who is measuring the slide ladder with a measuring tape and recording it in a notebook.

Over on another sheltered patio, children are moving freely from the inside to the outside. There is one child with an easel and paints; two children are making birdhouses at the woodworking bench. A six-year-old girl is sitting on the patio writing about bugs in a notebook. Three older children are sitting at the brightly painted round table (once used for telephone wire) playing a math game.

From this patio you can see inside the classroom area, as you could from the other outside areas. As you walk into the room you get the same feeling of action and spontaneity that you did observing the children outside. There are few individual desks in the room. Instead, there are tables supporting what look like interest or learning centers. On one side of the room is an arts and crafts area. Two children are making animals out of juice cans and construction paper. In the adjacent corner is a math area, with measuring materials, several sets of Cuisenaire rods, and graph paper. Two boys are charting the weights of three baby guinea pigs born the week before. A third child who has tired of painting joins them in their task. There is a daybed near the math area. Two boys are stretched out drawing pictures of each other. In what looks to be a language arts center a woman, possibly a parent, is typing out a story dictated by two five-year-olds. In the reading corner an older child is reading to a younger one who is stretched out on an oval rug. You spot another mother near a science area holding a small, squirming infant while talking to a group of three or four children about baby mammals.

As you are looking around the room you are seeing children ages five to eight engaged in many different activities, some in groups, some alone. They are writing, reading, listening, talking, building, painting. They seem to be getting along extremely well. You suddenly feel something is missing—the teacher. As you search the room you see several adults interacting with the children. Which is the teacher? You are told by a polite five-year-old that "That is the teacher," the woman calmly writing on the blackboard, unattended. She turns at a request for her presence at a "tea party" prepared and served by a group of boys and girls and joins them with a smile.

What is this experience all about? What does it tell you about this classroom? It is an open classroom to be sure, but what does that mean? In essence, it is an environment in which teachers, parents, and children are finding their own ways of expressing and exploring what they have to offer each other. Everyone learns from everyone else. Each person is a facilitator of learning. There is a wealth of materials and experiences and the children are often given free choice instead of strict routines and lessons. In their play the children are learning. They are doing and understanding, not just memorizing facts. They are learning to be independent, to be self-motivated, to explore, to inquire, to discover. Most of all, these children are experiencing the joy of learning. It is hoped that this book will aid you in continuing to help young children find joy and challenge through open learning.

1 ORGANIZING FOR EFFECTIVE OPEN LEARNING

The American school system has been the subject of much bitter criticism recently. Herbert Kohl, John Holt, and Joseph Featherstone among others have said that schools are not reaching their goals and are not meeting the needs and interests of children. Charles Silberman's well-known characterization of the schools describes them as "grim, joyless places that are needlessly authoritarian and repressive—not because teachers and principals are stupid or venal, but because nobody ever asks *why*: *Why* the rules? or *Why* the curriculum?" [1]

These criticisms have drawn attention to problems in the schools. Changes are resulting in a more meaningful, more effective, and more pleasant and exciting environment for learning. The development and implementation of the open learning concept may lead us to that desired new and better state of education.

[1] Vincent R. Rogers, *Teaching in the British Primary School*. (New York: Macmillan Publishing Co., Inc., 1970), p. vi.

WHAT IS AN OPEN-LEARNING ENVIRONMENT?

The classroom characterized by open educational procedures does not have a single organizational method, nor does it narrowly define teachers' or children's behaviors [2]. Its development here in the United States has been greatly influenced by the British Infant Schools and their efforts at becoming "open." Joseph Featherstone talks about what is happening there with regard to "new ways of thinking about how young children learn, classroom organization, the curriculum, and the role of the teacher." [3]

Open learning is a humanistic and personalized approach that centers on developing responsibility for discovery learning in children. The teacher no longer teaches just by telling but instead facilitates or guides learning by providing an interesting and meaningful environment. Classroom organization is more informal and the curriculum emphasis is focused on integrating various subject areas to take advantage of the children's interests. It can best be understood by looking at the philosophy on which it is based.

PHILOSOPHY

British educators say their program got its impetus from American educators such as George Counts, John Dewey, and Harold Rugg. In America this humanistic educational movement was either smothered by the heavy-handed academic emphasis brought on by Sputnik or misinterpreted by some of its followers [4]. The movement has flourished in Britain and is based on a philosophy differing from traditional educational philosophies in its new beliefs about children, their learning, and the role played by the teacher.

On Children

Children are seen as competent, trustworthy, and desirous of learning [5]. When they are shown trust they respond with productive, positive, and enjoyable behavior [6]. The only time a child must be prodded to learn or rewarded or punished is when the goal of adults for him opposes the purposes he has for himself [7].

[2] Bernard Spodek, "Alternatives to Traditional Education," *Peabody Journal of Education*, 48 (January 1971), 143.

[3] Joseph Featherstone, "Schools for Children: What's Happening in British Classrooms," *The New Republic*, 157 (August 19, 1967), 17.

[4] Minnie P. Berson, "Inside the Open Classroom," *Childhood Education*, 7 (May 1971), 11.

[5] Spodek, op. cit., pp. 143–44.

[6] Barbara D. Day, "Open Education Comes of Age," *North Carolina Education*, 2 (September 1971), 16.

[7] Spodek, loc. cit.

Proponents of this philosophy realize that a child needs the freedom to choose his own work for individual pride, dignity, and integrity. The child's curriculum should reflect his interests, his needs, and his right to order his own learning [8].

The child's emotions also have a part in this setting. Emotions here are acknowledged and then can be coped with. It is the teacher's responsibility to help the child realize how to recognize and deal with his feelings [9].

On Learning

Learning in an open classroom environment emphasizes psychomotor, cognitive, and affective learning through many sensory and concrete materials [10]. The child learns by inquiry and discovery in his own way and at his own pace. His natural love of learning and curiosity can be focused when he is provided with personalized teacher guidance and an informal and responsive classroom environment based on his interests [11].

Bernard Spodek states two underlying assumptions about learning in an open classroom. First, "Learning takes place as a result of an individual's encounter with his environment." This indicates an active sort of learning where the child understands through observations, thought, and, last of all, verbalization. Second, ". . . learning is not linear." There are many ways a child can master a particular concept. The individual learning style assumes equal importance with the goals [12]. Thus play is a reasonable mode of learning. Expression is also emphasized in learning whether it be through writing, acting, drawing, or dancing. Teaching comes not just through the teacher but from assignment cards and other children whose understanding is furthered by teaching others [13].

On the Role of the Teacher

The classroom teacher's role has changed. There are no longer lecturers at the front of the class or fixed formal reading groups. These methods ignored individual learning styles and forced a single pattern of learning on groups resulting in ability grouping and "tracking." [14]

Her goal is to aid children in developing respect for others, a sense of responsibility, self-discipline, and independence in learning [15]. Her role is that of the facilitator of learning instead of the source of learning; the child himself is

[8] Charles H. Rathbone, "Assessing the Alternatives," *Childhood Education*, **47** (February 1971), 236.

[9]   Ibid. pp. 236–37.

[10] Day, loc. cit.

[11] Berson, op. cit. p. 12.

[12] Spodek, op. cit. p. 143.

[13] Ibid., p. 142.

[14] Featherstone, loc. cit., p. 20

[15] Day, op. cit., p. 14.

the source [16]. Her job is to provide experiences that will initiate the child's thinking [17]. She guides by the environment and materials she provides.

The teacher will be moving around throughout the day as are the children. She may work with an individual child, a pair, or a small group. Usually she will be on the physical level of the children, sitting in a small chair or on the floor [18].

The teacher in this role should not be interpreted as a passive observer. She constantly challenges, suggests, stimulates, prods, and demands what the child is capable of doing. Neither does the teacher abrogate authority. She is not hesitant to establish and enforce necessary rules [19].

COMPONENTS OF OPEN LEARNING

Certain characteristics are associated with open-learning programs. It should be remembered, however, that open learning is a philosophy rather than a set organizational pattern or a particular teaching method. Individual teachers and individual classes may adopt this philosophy in many ways. All components may be present in any particular open-education program.

It should also be emphasized that establishing a good open classroom is most successful when children and teachers are able to work into it gradually. Thus it may be that a teacher is working toward the goal of having a completely open classroom, but she may start the program with only a small degree of openness such as setting up one center, then another, until the learning area becomes a busy laboratory for children. After much careful planning she may have a program that is working successfully but still has not incorporated all the following components.

Multi-Aging

An open classroom may be "multi-aged" or organized into "vertical" or "family" grouping. All three terms describe situations in which children of several ages are grouped together in a single class. This allows children to group themselves in the classroom as they would outside of school—on the basis of personal compatibility, comparable skills, and common interests. Each child's educational program is personalized accordingly [20].

This procedure seems especially effective in early childhood programs. Younger children learn from older children, many of whom assume the role of "junior teachers." This help comes in academic and social areas and is quite useful in

[16] Ibid., p. 16.
[17] Joseph Featherstone, "Schools for Learning," *The New Republic*, **159** (December 21, 1968), 18.
[18] Berson, op. cit., p. 14.
[19] Vincent Rogers, "Vincent Rogers Answers Your Questions on Open Education," *Instructor*, **81** (August/September 1971), 18.
[20] Berson, op. cit., p. 14.

teaching about the open classroom itself. Also helpful is the fact that teachers do not have a totally new group of children each year. Time is not wasted in the beginning of the year getting acquainted with each child's abilities, needs, and interests. Children are able to proceed on their own level of learning more easily; they are neither held back from learning nor labeled as "slow" if they need more time [21].

Integrated Curriculum and Integrated Day

In an integrated day program, the teacher no longer works with the whole class or teaches one group while the others do quiet seat work, but the subjects are learned and taught simultaneously. If they desire, children can be active all of the time because the room is organized into learning centers [22]. The daily schedule is no longer sliced into certain blocks for certain subjects, but both time and subject fields are integrated.

Charles H. Rathbone says, "The prepared curriculum is no longer an end but rather a starting place for learning." The child is seen as the primary curriculum organizer; he brings his own concerns into the learning process so old "coverage" goals are no longer applicable [23]. Problems devised by teachers and children take precedence over textbook problems—for example, "How much water is lost from a leaky hose in the schoolyard?" [24] Since the child's interests are the basis for the curriculum, when he becomes absorbed, he is allowed to continue working as long as he wishes rather than having to stop to begin studying another subject.

With the integrated curriculum, children can be taught around an open-ended theme. Expression becomes a valuable tool of integration because children can describe their observations through pictures, words, and movement [25].

This approach requires much flexibility on the part of the teacher. Students may respond to a problem or activity in a different way than had been anticipated. Therefore the teacher must be ready to adjust her plans or extend or drop a unit according to the children's responses [26].

Physical Organization into Centers

A visitor to the open classroom may feel at first that the atmosphere is confusing because the children are busy and active, the teacher does not dominate the atmosphere, and the classroom is arranged into nooks and crannies [27].

Much that is ordinarily thought of as necessary class equipment is not needed,

[21] Featherstone, "Schools for Children," p. 21.
[22] Berson, loc. cit.
[23] Rathbone, op. cit. p. 236.
[24] Featherstone, "Schools for Learning," p. 18.
[25] Berson, op. cit., p. 14.
[26] Rogers, op. cit., p. 75.
[27] Berson, loc. cit.

such as the teacher's desk and individually assigned children's desks [28]. The large space resulting from the removal of traditional necessities allows rooms to be decentralized and space to be divided into flexible and functional areas [29]. This can be accomplished through architectural design, demountable and movable partitions, and movable furniture [30].

If possible, the room should have rugs or mats to allow working on the floor. Also needed for working are large flat areas and student storage spaces. Planning should allow space adaptable for group sessions as well as individual work. Teachers will need a separate area for planning which might also be used for storage.

Open education philosophies have also extended the definition of the physical classroom into new areas. Classroom doors are left open to allow for a flow of activity into the outdoor learning environment [31] or to the hallways [32]. The library and media center have also become extensions of the classroom. They are seen as resource centers as well as areas for exploration and instruction [33].

The flexible planning and furnishings that make up the open classroom allow for the establishment of learning centers or areas. Materials in these centers will include commercial and teacher-made items as well as "junk" that will be used by the children for measuring, touching, collage, and in many other individual ways. There may be present many materials from the traditional class such as textbooks, workbooks, films, tapes and records, but they will be used as the individual needs them; they are part of, but not the entire, curriculum [34]. New materials will also be present such as learning task cards, self-corrective games, and teaching machines.

In arranging the learning centers, thought should be given to such factors as accessibility to sink, necessity for quiet atmosphere, and accessibility to patio and outdoor areas for activities that could be moved outside. As an example of one plan, Investigation and Fine Arts centers need to be near a sink. The Block Center, Home-Living, and Creative Dramatics Center are grouped near each other, as those are noisier activities. The woodworking materials need to be stored near the Block Center so that they can be easily moved onto the patio area during the day as can easels or the other art equipment. The Sand and Water Play Center can also be kept near the Science Center and moved out onto the patio during the day.

The Communication or Language Arts Center requires a more quiet atmosphere. This should be a very private area, perhaps, with individual study carrels, comfortable lounging areas supplied with big pillows, and maybe some small

[28] Featherstone, "Schools for Learning," p. 19.

[29] Day, loc. cit.

[30] Edwin W. MacBeth, "When the Walls Come Tumbling Down," *School Management*, 15 (August, 1971), 10–11.

[31] Day, loc. cit.

[32] Featherstone, "Schools for Children," p. 17

[33] MacBeth, op. cit., p. 9.

[34] Rogers, loc. cit.

rocking chairs. Tables for working should be dispersed throughout the room.

Some larger areas also should be left open so that space will be available for group discussions and sharing. For such times children could sit on the floor or perhaps on an arrangement of boards and bricks that the children could paint and decorate.

The plan given above is designed for a "pod" type organization with team teaching and several classes. A classroom in an older building could be similarly designed after walls were torn down (or even left as one self-contained open classroom) and doors cut leading to outside areas. This classroom could extend its boundaries by using the hallways for displays of collections leading to all kinds of reading, writing, or art, or possibly for a reading area.

USE OF CONTRACTS AND SELF-CORRECTIVE MATERIALS IN THE OPEN CLASSROOM

What Is a Contract?

Rita and Kenneth Dunn define a contract as "a prescription . . . written for, by, or with the student. It provides many opportunities for the youngster to learn independently and ideally includes a variety of learning resources (tapes, records, books, films, pictures, loops, slides, games, etc.) through which he may gather the required information." [35] With contracting, the child and teacher agree upon a certain quality and quantity of work that should be completed by a certain time. The child then works at his own pace. Once the contract is completed, the teacher and child evaluate how effectively the child has met his objectives [36].

Before contracting begins, diagnosis is necessary. This allows both teacher and child to be familiar with the child's abilities and skills in the area of discussion. The diagnosis may result from prior test performance, general observation, a pretest, or any other available sources [37].

Contracts should be negotiated so as to assure skill development but must include sufficient known skills to assure success. Contracts based on a particular student interest or on a "reward" can deviate completely from traditionally thought of school activities. At the same time, however, the teacher must keep in mind each student's overall plan of progress [38].

In determining contract styles the teacher needs to observe and consider such

[35] Rita Dunn and Kenneth Dunn, *Practical Approaches to Individualizing Instruction*: *Contracts and Other Effective Teaching Strategies* (West Nyack, N.Y.: Parker Publishing Co., Inc., 1972), p. 41.

[36] Robert M. Wilson and Linda B. Gambrell, "Contracting—One Way to Individualize," *Elementary English*, **50** (March 1973), 427.

[37] Ibid.

[38] James W. Stewart and Jack Shank, "Student–Teacher Contracting: A Vehicle for Individualizing Instruction," *Audiovisual Instruction*, **18** (January 1973), 32.

individual characteristics as maturity, independence, interests, and abilities [39].
Other factors to take into account are the child's attention span; sources of motivation such as self, rewards, teacher expectation or recognition of achievement; preferred physical conditions and environment such as library, learning centers, home, outside, hallways, carpet, floor, desk, table; most effective type of assignment whether teacher-selected tasks, mutually planned experiences, or totally self-directed activities. Of primary importance is a consideration of the child's perceptual strengths and styles and whether he responds best to sound recordings, tactile experiences, visual materials, kinesthetic activities, printed media, or multimedia contracts. With these factors in mind, the teacher must necessarily differentiate and individualize children's contracts.

Students should also be provided with group activities. These might include cooperative project ventures, peer-centered discussions, sharing information and perceptions, and group decision-making [41].

The principle underlying contracting is that children can learn better and more willingly if the learning is mutually planned by the teacher and child [42]. For this reason contract conferences are important in planning, reinforcement, and evaluation [43]. The teacher should remember that some children may need more guidance than others. She will be responsible to help children learn how to plan, carry out, and evaluate [44].

The contract should include the learning objectives, the necessary conditions and tasks needed for the learning activity, provisions for applying the skills or knowledge gained, and methods for evaluation [45]. Since time required for completion of the contract may differ according to the child, the specific activity, the amount of work, or the subject, the time element may also be negotiated [46].

What Are Self-Corrective Materials?

Self-corrective materials include any devices that are self-directive and have been made self-correcting so that the child can work successfully and independently with a minimum of teacher assistance. Materials should vary according to skills emphasis and level of difficulty. Some system of filing and color-coding would be particularly useful to children working independently [47].

Materials can be teacher-made or commercial. If commercial materials are teacher-directed, the teacher may need to make them self-instructive by making

[39] Ibid.
[40] Dunn and Dunn, op. cit., pp. 29-30.
[41] Ibid., p. 145.
[42] Wilson and Gambrell, loc. cit.
[43] Stewart and Shank, op. cit., p. 34.
[44] Wilson and Gambrell, loc. cit.
[45] Stewart and Shank, op. cit., p. 32.
[46] Wilson and Gambrell, op. cit., p. 428.
[47] Delwyn G. Schubert, "Individualized Self-Directed Correction," *Elementary English*, **50** (March 1973), 442.

directions simpler and by providing answers for self-checking. Care must be taken to make all directions specific and to gear them to the child's independent reading level [48]. With very young children a combination of pictures and words is helpful.

Skill and content teaching and enrichment can be accomplished by assembling and mounting materials clipped from old workbooks, Weekly Readers, children's magazines, and newspapers. The age approach is excellent and can be used to overcome specific weakness [49].

Other devices that are costly but good additions to a program of this sort are the EFI Audio Flashcard System, the Language Master, and the Borg-Warner System 80. Less costly would be an electric board that provides a lighted circuit or buzz when the student matches the correct question and answer [50].

Teachers can make materials self-directive by (1) writing answers on the backs of exercises; (2) writing answers upside down on the same paper in a place a bit removed from the questions; (3) using a flap that can be folded back to cover answers; (4) writing answers on a card that is put in a library card holder; (5) writing answers on cards kept in an answer file box [55].

Some teachers may raise the question of cheating when children are given answers. This probably will not result to a significant degree if the emphasis is on learning instead of testing. In minimal occasions where this does occur, learning will result from the associations that will be made [52].

Children may primarily find the open classroom a delightful but confusing environment. In the average situation adult supervision in each center all the time will be impossible. A child may have problems becoming familiar enough with the materials to find what he wants and what he needs. A program in the medial stages of development may experience difficulties in directing children to a variety of activities. Contracting is a useful and valid means of dealing with these problems.

Through the individualization of contracts, learning can proceed on levels appropriate to each individual's ability. Self-pacing is also made possible. The system prevents faster students from being bored and reduces frustration, anxiety, and boredom for slower students. The children may work individually or in teams with others who work at a similar pace.

The system is more motivating for students. Contracts take into consideration the child's interests and are planned around his abilities to make the venture successful. Contracting gives the child a choice in the learning process and substance. It gradually allows the child to develop personal responsibility for his learning [53]. Fullfillment of the contract leads to feelings of pride and self-esteem as a learner [54]. Certainly motivating is the one-to-one relationship

[48] Ibid.
[49] Ibid., pp. 442–443.
[50] Ibid., p. 443.
[51] Ibid., p. 442.
[52] Ibid.
[53] Dunn and Dunn, op. cit., p. 80.
[54] Wilson and Gambrell, op. cit., p. 429.

that develops between the teacher and student [55]. The system increases learning as well as self-concept [56].

When contracting makes some use of self-correcting materials, the child can proceed largely independently. He gains immediate reinforcement and correction, and learning becomes more purposeful and evident. The independence developed also helps the teacher. She is freed for individual instruction and discovers that the problem of classroom control diminishes when children are experiencing success [57].

Accountability is presently seen as a major trend in American education. Contracting provides a means for accounting to parents for what children are doing and where they are going. This is often important in gaining the endorsement by and cooperation of parents for the open classroom. It also gives the children a way to account to themselves.

Contract Explanations

A Curriculum Contract

A curriculum contract is essentially a single topic or unit that has been outlined by the teacher for the whole class. Each child may receive a copy and will use it as a basis for his individual contract, restricting or expanding it according to his academic abilities and learning style.

Dunn and Dunn present this outline for a curriculum contract:

1. Behavioral objectives written for the child that explain:
    a. What the child must learn
    b. How the child can demonstrate that he has learned the specified information, applications, skills, etc.
    c. The degree of proficiency expected of the child
2. Media resources alternatives
3. Activity alternatives
4. Reporting alternatives [58].

(See Chapter 6, "Investigation in Science and Mathematics," A Sample Contract on Seeds, pp. 113-114.)

A widely used derivation of the curriculum contract is what the author of the present book has chosen to call an individual skill area contract. This type of contract involves the negotiation of objectives, activities, resources, expected proficiency, and evaluation procedures. The teacher and child would negotiate a contract to develop or refine a particular skill or skill area such as spelling or vowel sounds. Thus a child might be working on several contracts for various areas during one time period. Each contract might last from a day to two weeks.

[55] Stewart and Shank, loc. cit.
[56] Ibid., p. 34.
[57] Wilson and Gambrell, loc. cit.
[58] Dunn and Dunn, op. cit. p. 79.

(See Chapter 2, "Communications: The Language Arts," A Sample Contract on Vowels, p. 54.)

When a class or student begins to work by a system of contracting, the teacher will select and organize the content of the contract. Student options will include negotiation of due dates and sequence of learning activities.

Later, student options grow as students become more familiar with the contracting procedure and demonstrate more responsibility. Students may have a larger voice in planning the contract or they may work from teacher objectives and draft their own contracts. Options may grow through the introduction of the reward contract. In this case the previous major contract specifies the content of the reward contract. It may be totally student-planned or may be chosen by the teacher based on her knowledge of the student's interests. Another possibility is an expansion of the duration of the contract [59].

An Independent Contract

Some children may need a contract that differs from the typical curriculum contract. These children may have a special problem or need that makes the required basic curriculum inappropriate or ineffective for them [60]. They need an intense internal motivation and need a contract that is totally built on the child's interests [61]. Such a child might have severe reading problems or be extremely hyperactive but have a great interest in animals around which his program could be organized. The theory behind this is that once the child experiences successful learning in a field of his interest, he will be motivated to succeed in other fields of learning. (See Chapter 6, "Investigation in Science and Mathematics," A Sample Contract on Baby Animals, pp. 114-115.)

The Daily Contract

The daily contract is a variation of contracting adopted for the open classroom by many teachers. It specifies where a child should go and what he should do in several centers and usually leaves him some time for free choices. This is seen as a method to help children investigate various centers and various materials as well as work on specific needs.

It may be expanded to a contract covering several days. It may lead to a reward contract when the child may spend his whole day working on one particular area of interest. The daily contract may include such useful features as provision for student evaluation or provision for meeting with the teacher on an individual or group basis. (See Chapter 12, "Evaluating and Recording Open Learning," pp. 177-192.)

[59] Stewart and Shank, op. cit., p. 32.
[60] Dunn and Dunn, op. cit., p. 124.
[61] Ibid., p. 126.

CONCLUSION

An open environment, then, is one that can successfully meet the needs of children and make learning a more meaningful and joyful experience. The factor that determines success or failure in this program is the teacher's conviction in the open learning philosophy. She must adapt the system to her teaching style and her beliefs about children and learning so that she feels comfortable and capable. Her attitude is crucial for it affects and shapes the psychological environment for the group of children. The teacher must view each child as a human being, unique from all others. She must realize that each child is motivated in different ways, reacts differently to stimuli, and in turn learns in different ways and at differing rates. Thus a child–centered learning environment is essential. If the child is the "raison d'etre" of schools, then he must be the central focus for the teacher and the learning environment.

The physical arrangement of the learning environment should consist of a variety of learning centers containing a wide and varied assortment of materials that are both self-corrective and open-ended. An ideal situation would be a unit of teachers employing team teaching and multi-aging. This situation would be advantageous in supplying a larger area to provide more centers and more equipment for the children. This situation would also provide more supervision in the various centers and would capitalize on the strengths of each teacher. As stated previously, however, the physical facility does not determine openness; it facilitates it. Obviously, open learning can occur in a self-contained open-learning environment. There is no one arrangement that is best or prescribed for all teachers. Teachers and children must work to find out the best organizational plan for their learning and working together, depending upon the physical space available. Whatever the arrangement of learning centers may be, open learning necessitates a well-organized environment where children respect materials and use them in a meaningful way, and where the care of this environment and the appropriate storage of materials are dependent upon all who work and learn there. For very young children the materials may need to be color-coded according to the various learning centers. These centers must be changed, expanded, and contracted in order to provide for continuous growth of the children. All available space should be utilized for learning, both inside and out-of-doors.

Open learning occurs in a healthy and trusting social environment, where children retain their individuality while participating as a member of a large social group. Both individual and group interests are held in high esteem by all. A child learns from everything around him, including other people, therefore, it is most important that his school be a place where children live good social attitudes. It must be a place where they learn internal self-discipline through positive social values—a place where teachers, through time spent with individuals, are able to develop feelings of personal worth in each child.

An open-learning environment further emphasizes an integrated approach to curriculum and instruction, where children are given an opportunity to explore, select from, and react to a rich and varying environment that is well planned, inviting, encouraging, and challenging. A balance of intellectual, social, emotional, physical, and aesthetic growth is provided for each child. The interests of children stem from the kinds of learning materials available to them. The curriculum is reflected in the learning environment through the careful planning of teachers and based on the needs and interests of children whom the teachers know so well. The teacher's instructional goals must be clear to her, yet provide flexibility for children to engage in activities that are genuinely rewarding for them. Learning skills in various subject areas go on simultaneously while the children work in a variety of learning centers.

Such an open-learning approach provides many advantages and answers to questions asked for years by educators and children alike. The author's reaction is best expressed by a statement made by John Holt: "The time has come to do something very different. The way to begin is—to begin." [62] I hope that *Open Learning in Early Childhood* will enable those who work with young children to do just that—and much more.

[62]   John Holt, *What Can I Do Monday?* (New York: E. P. Dutton and Company 1970), p. 3.

2 BLOCKS

Blocks have been standard equipment in nursery schools and kindergartens for many years; yet they afford many learning opportunities in the primary grade. Success or failure of this center is usually correlated with the role the teacher plays. As a facilitator of learning, she must "set the stage" by providing the necessary raw materials, a watchful eye, a listening ear, skillful questions, and suggestions to lead the child's thinking and constructing to new avenues of concept development.

Environmental Resources

Storage space and cabinets to house blocks
Define space for building construction
Rug—to reduce noise
Set of solid wooden blocks
    Unit blocks (approx. 1 1/2″ × 3″ × 5″)
    Double unit blocks
    Quadruple unit blocks
    Ramps
    Curves (elliptical 1/2 and 1/4)
    Curves (circular 1/2 and 1/4)
    Y shapes
    Triangles
    Cylinders
Set of hollow blocks—varying in size

Other Building and Block Materials

Tinker Toys
Lincoln Logs
Large- and small-wheel toys—airplane,
    trucks, trains, tractors, etc.
Rubber animals (zoo and farm)
Small plastic people
Rubber people (farmer, policeman, etc.)
Puppets

Planks
Tiles
Packing crates, boxes, ropes
Old steering wheel
Traffic signs
Books related to building
Pencil for labeling

Teacher-made Materials and Suggestions

1. *Block Cart.* Using a wooden crate, add wheels and a handle. This will make an excellent cart for the children to move the blocks outside.
2. *Milk Carton Blocks.* Cut off the pouring end of two milk cartons. Put one inside of the other. These will make good hollow blocks. Use 1/2 pint, pint, quart, and 1/2 gallon cartons.
3. *Blocks from Wood Scraps.* Sand and varnish or paint scrap 2 × 4 bits of wood from a construction site.
4. *Block Area.* Mark off the block area by using masking tape on the floor.
5. *Alphabet Blocks.* Print the numerals or letters of the alphabet on small blocks. Use them for math or spelling.
6. *Geometrical Shapes.* With a jigsaw and a piece of plywood, cut out various shapes (stars, circles, squares, etc.). Let children match the shape and the hole.
7. *Responsible Clean-up.* To assist children in putting the blocks away either draw a large diagram of the shelves where various blocks go to hang above the shelves, or trace the outline of the various blocks on the shelves and paint them.

Some Objectives

To enjoy the block area by working with the blocks for fun.

To improve small and large muscle coordination by working with and building with blocks.

To role-play with the animals, people, and/or puppets.

To learn to share ideas and work together in a group while taking turns with the blocks.

To develop concepts of big, little, more than, less than, equal to, shapes and sizes.

To use materials to create the child's world as he sees it.

To be able to express himself nonverbally and to release emotions in an acceptable form.

To explore the dynamics of balance through construction.

Suggested Activities

1. *Map Study*. Use blocks for defining map study. Children might take a walk around the block or the school community, return to school, and use blocks to make a model of what they saw. (*Examples*: streets, paths, buildings, shopping center or stores, trees, church, etc.)

2. *Bridge*. After a visit to a river (or a film on rivers), some children might be interested in constructing a bridge, boats, etc.

3. *Role Play*. Children might make puppets in the art area to use for role play in the block center. These might be added to cars, boats, or airplanes made in the woodworking center.

4. *Correlation with Science*. When inquiry or discussions lead to simple machines, a book on their use and construction might be added to the center, and the simple machines placed in the center.

5. *A New Center*. A new center might be developed using ingenuity of the children and blocks (*Examples*: store, post office, etc.)

6. *Therapeutic Value*. The child may be able to work out emotions and frustrations using blocks, rubber animals, and rubber people.

7. *Low Enclosures*. Encourage children to construct low enclosures for imaginative eating, sleeping, etc.

8. *Task Cards*. Draw a picture of a particular construction on the card. Ask the child to copy the construction. Other cards might read:
   - Build a house and write a story about the people who live in it.
   - What did the house Hansel and Gretel find in the forest look like? Build it as you think it might look.
   - Think about the street you live on and the streets that go out from it. Draw a map. From the map, construct the neighborhood you live in. Someone who lives near you could help you do this.
   - Build a city or a town other than your own. Label some of the buildings. You might like to lay out the streets also, using the traffic signs.

Build an ⬆

Label it.

How many blocks
did you use? _____
Show it to 3 boys
and 3 girls.

9. *Outside Block Play*. Move the blocks outside. Some of the large pieces from the center might remain out at all times. Outdoor space is more conducive to larger building of objects (forts, submarine, etc.).

10. *Temporary Constructions*. Have a pile of scrap lumber outside the classroom for building temporary constructions in the out-of-doors. Children can build something much larger outside than they can inside.

11. *Experience Stories*. Help the child label constructions and encourage him to dictate, tape, type, or write a story about the construction.

12. *Road Strips*. Small transportation models encourage children to build roads. The children can lay out road strips to form routes, tracks, etc.

13. *Poems, Pictures, Books, Objects*. Poems, pictures, books, and objects appropriately displayed in the block center can be used to initiate creative construction.

   Examples:

   Pictures—Pictures of small boats or planes may invite the building of harbors, docks, or airfields.

   Poems—A short poem about a haunted castle or a king and queen might invite castle building.

   Books—Books on transportation might initiate the desire for a bus or train terminal.

   Objects—Rubber animals might invite children to build a zoo.

14. *Tiles*. Provide tiles of all shapes, sizes, and colors so the children can make floors for models if they desire. Tile can also be used to designate building parts, land from sea, paths, roads, etc.

15. *Small-Scale Constructions*. Lincoln logs, Tinker Toys, and other sets and kits can be used to do small-scale construction on a table or a designated floor area. (These can be easily stored.)

3 COMMUNICATION: THE LANGUAGE ARTS

The language arts field is the world of code-breaking processes that opens the doors of oral and written communication. A learning environment that supports and encourages communication should be filled with materials for listening, viewing, reading, writing, and speaking. Stimulating the growth of oral and written language as well as creative thought is especially important, for while everyone is not a poet or a great teller of tales, each and everyone, when encouraged, can write or tell something. The success of this center lies in finding out what interest the child holds and then building on that interest.

Environmental Resources

1-2 tables and 2-4 chairs each
Small table with typewriter
Low shelves used also as a divider
Rocking chair, easy chairs, couch
Carpet, rug, or carpet squares
Pillows or floor cushions
Book rack
Open storage for records, tapes, etc.
Carrels for individual usage
Electrical outlets

Writing Materials

Paper—lined, plain white paper, construction paper of various colors, shapes and
sizes; chart paper, index cards, canary second sheets
Pencils, crayons, water colors, magic markers, scissors, and other equipment
necessary for making individual books and stories
Pictionaries, dictionaries, and a high-frequency word list
Picture file, story starter file (mounted pictures for writing about titles, stories,
and words)
Photographs (current snapshots of children and activities)
Books with blank pages and open-ended titles
Chalkboard; white and various colors of chalk
Mailbox
Book jackets
Word boxes

Reading Materials

Books—child-made, high interest level (varying ability levels), paperbacks, and
comics
Books with coordinating records or tapes
Books with coordinating filmstrips
Stories—child-written and commercial
Talk-starter picture cards
Puppets
Flannel board with flannel objects, labels, letters, story characters
Magnetic board, letters
Lotto games
Matching picture and letter games
Parquetry blocks, designs
Puzzles—variety of topics and number of pieces
Spelling and reading games
Crossword puzzles

Resource books such as children's encyclopedias, science library, Childcraft
Newspapers—class, local, and city (current)
Magazines (popular as well as children's)
Catalogs
Tapes—blank, teacher-made, and commercially prepared

Viewing and Listening Equipment

Language Master, 101, and other language experience machines
Record player and records
Tape recorder and tapes (regular and/or casette)
Super-8 projector and film loops
Slide, filmstrip, and picture viewers, filmstrips
Slide projector and slides
Earphones (8–12 separate or 2 sets of 6), jacks
Film projector and film
Screen
Overhead projector, transparencies (blank and prepared)
TV, radio, walkie-talkie
Programmed materials
Filmstrips with coordinating records
Camera and film

Teacher-made Materials

1. *Large Wooden Puzzles.* On a piece of 1/4″ plywood, paint a picture, character, etc. Draw off puzzle pieces. (Children will enjoy puzzle pieces shaped like an object such as a dog, cat, flower.) Use a jigsaw to cut the pieces.

2. *Lotto Games.* Lotto games can be made using starting sounds, animals, farm animals, objects, etc. Draw or use pictures from workbooks and mount on railroad board; laminate. Make four cards with twelve pictures on each card; make small squares of identical pictures.

3. *Learning Task Cards.* Laminated cards can be used for many purposes in this center: story starters, completion of a story (cartoons with dialogue cut out which children can supply), skills cards, or for suggested ideas to do in the center.

4. *Classification Games.* Use pictures from magazines, books, workbooks, etc. Mount them on railroad board; laminate. Construct cardboard pocket chart. Make small cards with pictures corresponding to categories on pocket chart. Examples of categories are toys, foods, animals, clothes, people, furniture, etc.

5. *Laminated Pictures.* Cut out interesting pictures from magazines, etc. Laminate them and use as talk or story starters.

6. *Sequence Cards.* Cut out logical series of pictures. (Comic strips are excellent.) Laminate them on separate pieces of tagboard. Have children put together in sequential order. The number may be placed on the back of the cards as a self-checking method. Suggest to the child that he write a story to go with the cards.

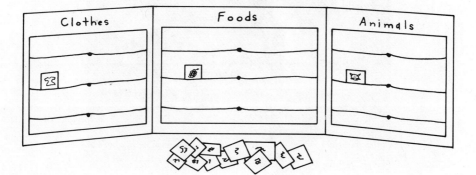

7. *Story or Talk Starter Cards.*   Laminate pictures on tagboard and place a sentence starter on it.   *Example*:   "The fox was on his way to see the chicken when . . . "

8. *Rhyming Puzzles.*   Use colored tagboard and laminate.   Include rhyming words and pictures.   The activity is self-correcting.

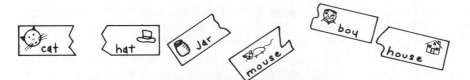

9. *Picture Files.* Contact a box. Fill it with mounted pictures on tagboard. Select pictures that are appealing to children. On some cards, include story starters and vocabulary words relevant to the pictures. Leave others with only pictures.

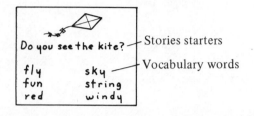

10. *Kinesthetic Letters.* Cut letters from sandpaper, corregated cardboard, or form with yarn. Glue letters on cardboard squares.
11. *ABC Dog.* Cut dog and letters from tagboard; laminate. Children can put together in order or use for letter recognition.

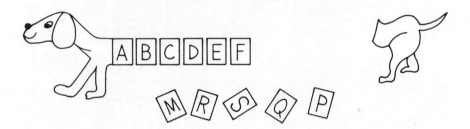

12. *Practice Writing Cards.* Cut tagboard to fit duplicating machine and make a stencil of handwriting lines. Run paper through machine one sheet at a time. Place square containing upper- and lower-case letter and picture of object with the initial sound of the letter on each card. Use magic marker to show formation of letters using arrows and numbers. Laminate. Children use erasable pens to practice letters. You can also put basic vocabulary words on back of card for children to practice writing.

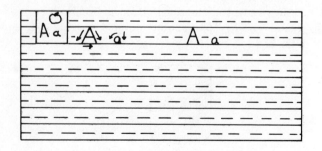

13. *Puppets.* Make hand, finger, bag, or sock puppets.

14. *Folders of Ideas.* Use file folders to contain activities for skill development. Use Baggies or stapled acetate to hold object. Write directions on folders. These can be adapted for many skills (rhyming words, syllables, blends, finger puppets, etc.).

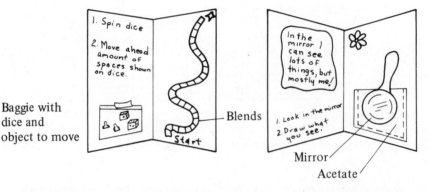

15. *Sand or Salt Trays.* Buy pans and plastic covers (baking pans can be purchased at variety stores). Cover bottom 1/2″ deep with sand or salt. (Salt cleans up more easily if spilled.)

16. *Feel Box.* Use an interesting box such as a large ice cream container. Cut round hole in side of container and attach the upper part of a sock for children to reach through. Have another covered opening large enough to place objects in the box.

17. *Cardboard Carpentry Storage Cabinet.* Cardboard carpentry carrels such as the ones shown can be readily made for classroom use. These can be used for individual study, or for storage. (Remove the top and bottom for use as carrels.)

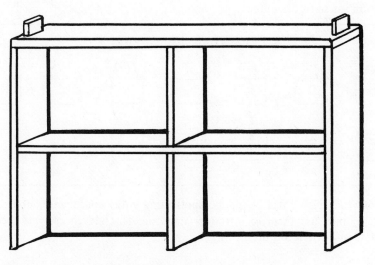

18. *TV.* Cut a rectangle in the back of a cardboard box. Cut holes for dowel rods to fit into both sides of the TV. Draw a continuous action story on a roll of paper. Staple paper to dowels in a scroll–like fashion, after the rolls have been placed in the TV. Caption for the TV might read: "Become a TV script writer. Write your own dialogue for this story." "Instead of drawing your own story, you might cut out stories from comic books, or from magazines."

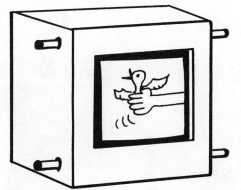

19. *Film Stage.* Show filmstrip into box painted black with inside back wall painted white, or use white construction paper in back.
20. *Language Master or 101 Machine Cards.* Although commercial cards are available for these machines, children will respond enthusiastically to cards made by the teacher which pertain to things they are currently interested in.

21. *Alphabet Pockets*. Use a large piece of tagboard (flannel board, material wall hanging, etc.) with alphabet pockets. Glue pictures on construction paper that will fit into pockets. Sort pictures into alphabet pocket which has on it the letter that begins that word. Correct letter is on the back of each picture for self-correction.

22. *Sound Puppets*. Make puppets representing initial consonant sounds. The teacher may use them to introduce new sounds; children can use them as follow-up activity on their own.

23. *Tagboard Alphabet Puzzle Pieces*. Use colored tagboard and laminate. Match upper-case alphabet letter with lower-case letter. Pieces will not fit unless matched correctly.

24. *Sound Task Cards*. Use colored tagboard and laminate. Grease pencil can then be used.

25. *Rhyming Words Hat.* Children can pull strip through the hat as they make and say the rhyming words.

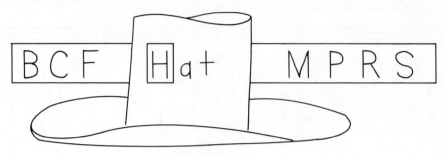

Felt Hat on Tagboard

26. *Rhyming Words Fan.* Children can pull the strip through the fan as they make and say the rhyming words.

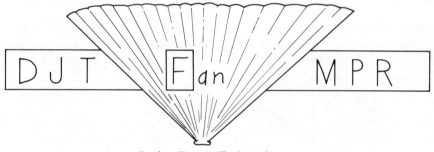

Burlap Fan on Tagboard

27. *Task Cards for Opposites.* The task cards can be made with tagboard and laminated for durability. Colored shoelaces (or yarn) are used for lacing. The lace color matches the color on the back of card for self-correcting.

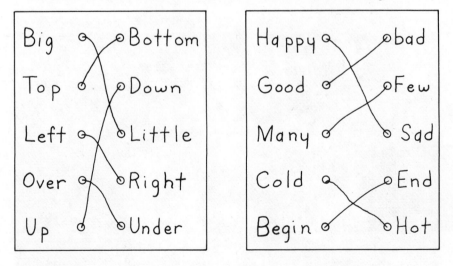

28. *Sentence Makers*. Write sentences on sentence strips. Make about ten or twelve. Divide the sentences midway (preferably between subject and predicate). Mix the sentence parts. The students are to match the segments to make complete sentences.

29. *Footprints*. Make a colorful set of footprints. Left feet have upper-case alphabet letters; right feet, lower-case. The children arrange them in order across the room, or in circles, etc.

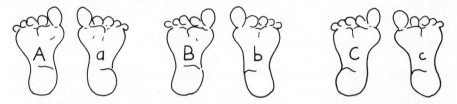

30. *"Ick Ack Ock."* Cut three roof-shaped peaks along the top of a sheet of tagboard. In each peak write the letter or letters for a sound being studied in phonics. Cut rows of triangular slots in each house. Cut squares of tagboard for each slot. Draw a picture containing one of the sounds on the roof on each card.

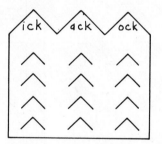

31. *Matching Rhyming Words*. Rule two pieces of tagboard into nine squares each. Draw a picture in each square of the first sheet. For each picture on the first sheet, draw a rhyming picture on the second sheet. Cut the pictures on the second sheet into separate cards. Put the cards in an envelope and clip the envelopes to the first, uncut sheet.

32. *Sound Puzzles*. Each puzzle has three parts. First, child recognizes sound of first two pictures; next, tries to find piece with letter associated with this sound; last, finds another with picture of the sound. There is a puzzle for each letter of the alphabet.

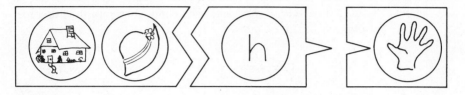

33. *Indian Blends*. Board game with set of cards telling child to make a word with a certain beginning blend and how many spaces he may move. Some cards refer to *certain animals* along path to which child must move. Game may be oriented to rhyming words, vowel words, or other skill concept by making new sets of cards.

34. *Vowel Cards*. Deck of forty cards with words and pictures of long and short vowel sounds (four for each). Can be used for various card games such as "Go Fishing," or deck can be divided and used for "Concentration."

35. *The Alphabet Worm.* Make a chart like the one shown. Make 27 circles to correspond with the circles on the worm for the children to match.

36. *Mrs. Long and Mr. Short.* Make cards with long and short vowel sounds. Place the words in a box. The children are to read the words and place them in the pockets of Mrs. Long or Mr. Short.

37. *Color Chart and Days of the Week Chart.* Make word cards, one for each color, to be placed in pockets on the Color Chart, and word cards, one for each day of the week, to be placed in pockets on the Days of the Week Chart.

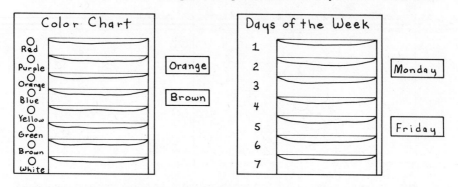

38. *Make a Story.* Write a story on sentence strips. Mix up and clip together. The students arrange the strips in order.

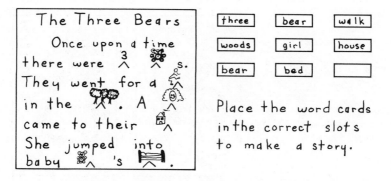

Place the word cards in the correct slots to make a story.

39. *Climb the Haystack.* Mount on a large piece of colorful tagboard and laminate. Using a wax pencil, the student may write the missing letters directly on the laminated tagboard.

Can you climb this haystack?

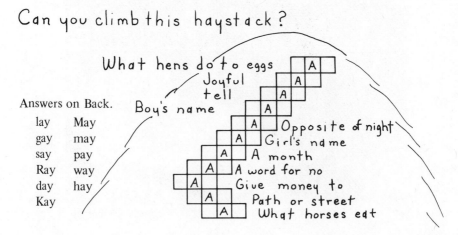

What hens do to eggs
Joyful
tell
Boy's name
Opposite of night
Girl's name
A month
A word for no
Give money to
Path or street
What horses eat

Answers on Back.

lay	May
gay	may
say	pay
Ray	way
day	hay
Kay	

40. *Initial Consonant Puzzle Pieces*. Use colored tagboard and laminate. Match picture with beginning consonant sound. Pieces will not fit unless correctly matched.

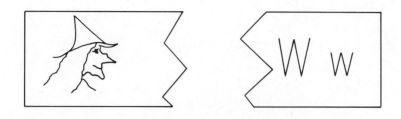

41. *Contraction Wheel*. Use colored tagboard and laminate. Match contraction clothespins with word pairs on the wheel. Make it self–correcting by placing answers on the back of the wheel and clothespins.

42. *Compound Word Wheel*. This can be made with laminated tagboard. Clothespins are made to match with a word on the tagboard, thus making it a compound word. (The same sort of wheels can be made for antonyms, synonyms, and homonyms.)

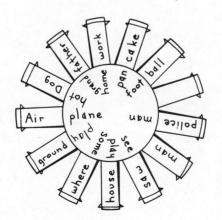

43. *Vowels Wheels.* Use colored tagboard and laminate. Students may use a wax crayon or nonpermanent magic marker to *draw a line to the vowels and to the words that have long and short vowel sounds.* Answers are placed on the back of each wheel.

A. *Vowels*

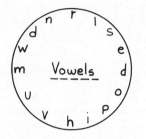

B. *Long Vowel Sounds*

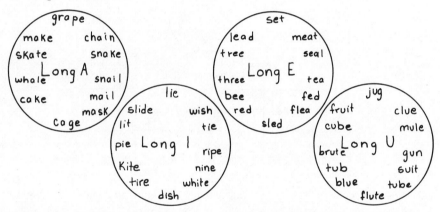

C. *Short Vowel Sounds*

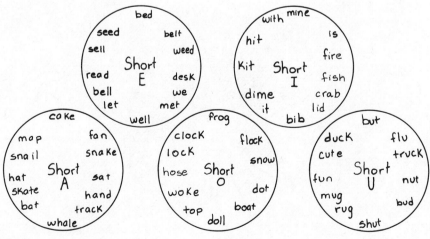

44. *Bingo*. Use colored tagboard and laminate for durability. A student or the teacher may call the game using ABC or word cards. In order to get bingo the student must fill five spaces horizontally, vertically, diagonally, or four corners. The winner gets to call the next game.

Y y	I i	W w	Q q	S s
C c	M m	E e	L l	V v
K k	R r	Free	A a	P p
G g	T t	N n	U u	J j
B b	H h	F f	O o	X x

to	this	like	up	look
funny	and	title	is	run
are	you	Free	red	go
he	come	of	the	play
see	can	said	my	jump

Tuesday	week	Thursday	Month	Day
Sunday	Saturday	June	September	March
May	February	Free	November	Friday
October	July	Time	April	year
Monday	January	August	Wednesday	December

45. *Prefix–Suffix Beanbag Toss.* Use oil cloth, a window shade, or a large piece of tagboard. The student should say a word containing the prefix or suffix in the block the beanbag lands on when thrown.

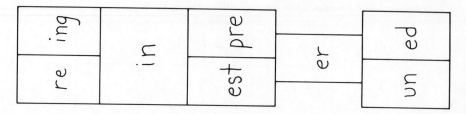

46. *Alphabet and Object Jars.* Collect small-sized baby food jars. In each jar, place an object (i.e., a nail, candle, dime, toy car, chalk, string, marble, lipstick, film, crayon, clip, paper, etc.). Make a label for each jar and place in a box or envelope. The children "label" the jars by placing the tags or cards on or in front of the jars. A variation is to place objects in 27 jars, each object beginning with a different letter of the alphabet. Place alphabet cards on the jars and arrange in alphabetical order.

47. *Sort-a-Long-Vowel and Sort-a-Short-Vowel.* Use an egg carton with a vowel in each holder. Student may sort picture or word cards into appropriate holders according to vowel sounds.

48. *Pick a Bundle from the Basket.* Place a wicker basket of bundles (made by using colorful laminated tagboard) in the writing center or perhaps on the floor in a reading nook. The bundles contain a variety of words taken from reading books or from appropriate areas of interest or projects ongoing in the learning area. Students may write a story using words on the bundles.

49. *Clever Clovers.* The clover can be made by using different colored laminated tagboard. Place them in a colorful box (covered with contact paper) in the writing center.

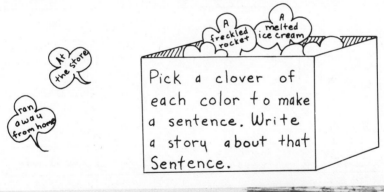

50. *Hang Out the Syllables*. Using a board (i.e., a material bolt, tri-wall cardboard, or laminated tagboard) attach envelopes or library card holders to make pockets. Children may sort word cards in the pockets by syllables.

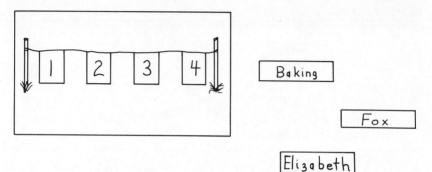

51. *Think-an-Action-Word*. Pictures showing action can be cut from magazines and glued on spaces drawn on tagboard and then laminated. Children may throw dice and move the designated number of spaces. If a student lands on one of the action pictures, he must say a verb that says what the picture shows.

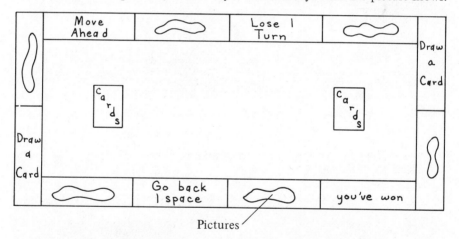

Pictures

52. *Glow-Worm*. Using at least eight colors of paper, make a worm with each section having a different color. Also, make matching sections, mounted on straws. These can be matched to the glow-worm sections. The color names may be printed on the back of each.

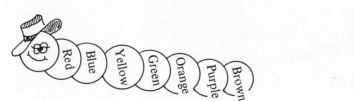

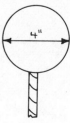

53. *Cups and Saucers*. Made with tagboard and pictures (either drawn free hand or from magazines), this game can be played by matching the cup and saucer with rhyming words, numerals with number words, words with long and short sounds, upper- and lower-case letters, etc. Answers can be placed on the backs for self-correction.

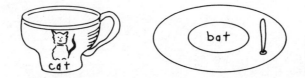

54. *Help the Rabbit Find His Tail*. The rabbit, word cards, and word tails can be made with tagboard and laminated. Several possible answers may be placed on the backs of the word cards and word tails. A student or small group of children can put together the rabbit and tails that make compound words.

55. *Rhyme Time*. Use cardboard covered with material or contact paper for the base of the game. Laminated tagboard may be used for the directions card and the word strips. A commercial spinner or one made with tagboard will be needed.

DIRECTIONS: RHYME TIME

Turn the spinner and make that number of moves on the board. If you can think of a word that rhymes with the one on the block, you take another turn.

hand	will	bin	ball	tell	fun
corn					rug
wet					can
hop					sit
night					not
take					so

| so | hope | lake | din | STOP |

| book | | | | | |
| big | house | red | shoe | boy | run | cat |

| tree | duck | fast |
| | | GO |

56. *Blends Race*. Use cardboard covered with material or contact paper for the base of the game. Colored, laminated tagboard may be used for the race track. Children can move tiny cars around the track, following the direction mounted on the board.

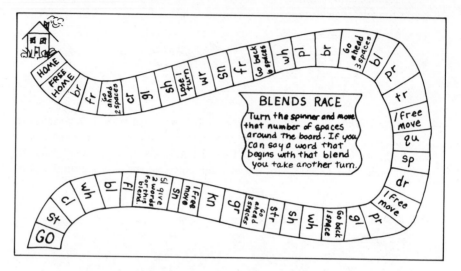

57. *What Kind of Sentence?* Use cardboard covered in colorful contact paper. Staple four library card holders or envelopes on the cardboard, three holders representative of a different kind of sentence and the fourth holder containing a variety of sentences. A child or small group of children may sort the sentences into the correct holder.

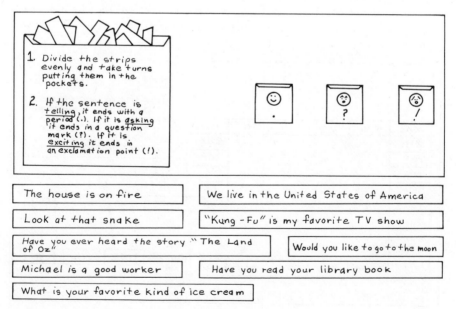

58. *Divide-O-Rule.* Use cardboard covered with contact paper and library card holders for Rules 1–4. The directions are explained on the game board. Make word strips for sorting into the holders or pockets. These may be stored in a brown envelope stapled to the back of the board.

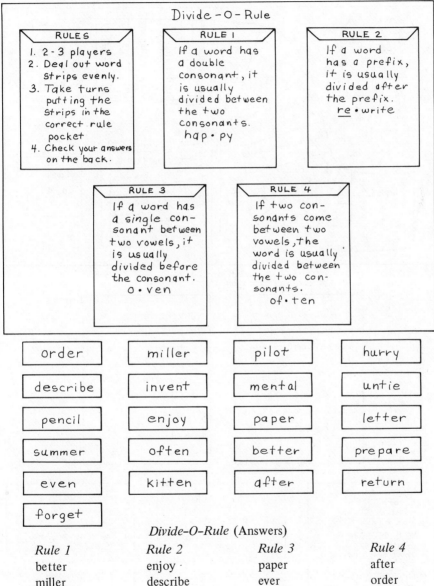

Divide – O – Rule

RULES
1. 2-3 players
2. Deal out word strips evenly.
3. Take turns putting the strips in the correct rule pocket
4. Check your answers on the back.

RULE 1
If a word has a double consonant, it is usually divided between the two consonants.
hap • py

RULE 2
If a word has a prefix, it is usually divided after the prefix.
re • write

RULE 3
If a word has a single consonant between two vowels, it is usually divided before the consonant.
o • ven

RULE 4
If two consonants come between two vowels, the word is usually divided between the two consonants.
of • ten

order · miller · pilot · hurry
describe · invent · mental · untie
pencil · enjoy · paper · letter
summer · often · better · prepare
even · kitten · after · return
forget

Divide-O-Rule (Answers)

Rule 1	*Rule 2*	*Rule 3*	*Rule 4*
better	enjoy ·	paper	after
miller	describe	ever	order
summer	untie	metal	forget
hurry	return	river	pencil
letter	prepare	pilot	often
kitten	invent		

59. *Land of Oz.* Use a piece of styrofoam or cardboard covered with colorful contact paper. Railroad board (laminated) may be used to make the yellow brick walk (with word on some of the bricks), Emerald City, the directions card, and the task cards. A small box may be used to hold the task cards.

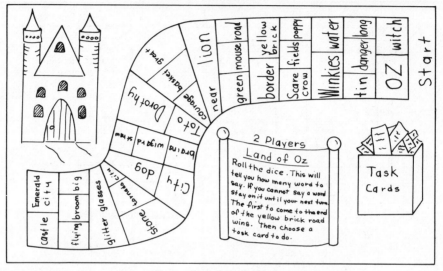

Examples of Task Cards

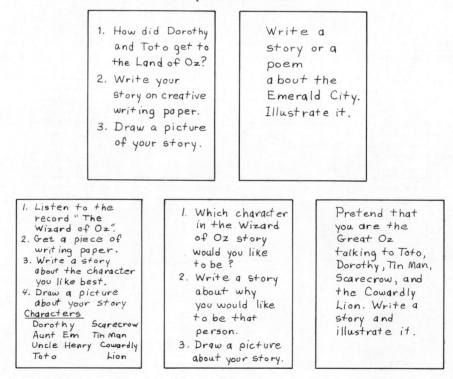

Some Objectives

To find success in working with the materials on his interest and developmental level.

To use resource materials for research related to other centers.

To be alone to think, to read, or to write.

To read and to be read to.

To dictate his ideas to others to be put in books.

To tell a story in proper sequence.

To communicate experiences in writing by adding ideas to incomplete books.

To use pictorial representation as his method of writing.

To make his own books using his own dialect, ideas, and illustrations.

To use the typewriter to find symbols to make his name, words, sentences.

To listen to words (or a story) while reading words (or story) silently while viewing a pictorial representation (*examples*: Language Master with pictorial card, Dukane, filmstrip, and record).

To enjoy using machines and to find new ways to use them more effectively.

To improve observation skills by observing film loops of interest.

To manipulate and use various equipment in different centers, alone, with a small group, or with the teachers.

Suggested Activities

1. *Experience Stories.* A child dictates to the teacher an experience and then the story is read by the child.
2. *Word Cards.* Teacher and/or child makes cards that have real meaning to the child. Cards are kept and the child reads them to the teacher as a follow-up.
3. *Creative Writing Box.* Laminated pictures with open-ended questions stimulate a child to write. These pictures are kept in a creative writing box.
4. *Story Starter File.* A file with index cards—color-coded by subject area—is used as a story starter. Each card has a title or a beginning paragraph of a story.
   Follow-up: The child can then write, dictate, or record his story on tape.
5. *Newspaper.* Small groups take turns reporting day's events. Editor of the day might use the typewriter to make the final copy.
6. *Photos.* Polaroid photos of children's current experiences stimulate children to verbalize and discuss sequence of events and perhaps to write about the event.
7. *Letters.* Felt, sandpaper, and/or wooden letters—teacher-made or commercial—can be used to trace, recognize shape and form, design, stencil, receive sensory pleasure, and to place on flannel board.

8. *Writing at the Chalkboard.* Encourage children to write or sketch on the board. You might put some kind of starting idea on the board such as: "What I Did Last Night," "A Funny Thing Happened to Me," "Draw Here . . ."

9. *Making Booklets*
   a. Use *comic strips.* Either erase wording for creative writing or leave for reading pleasure.
   b. Make books in *particular shapes*: "What Is Round?" "If I Were a Monster"
   c. *Compose books* in which all children have an opportunity to write: "My Favorite TV Show," "Our Families on Vacation," etc.

10. *Mailbox.* Place a mailbox in or out of classroom to encourage children to communicate in writing. Notes, invitations, thank-you's, get-well notes, etc., can go through this channel. Mail can get sent out through a classroom mail carrier.

11. *Idea Exchange Box.* Students write suggestions for interesting activities such as cooking experiences, science experiments, good books to read.

12. *Typewriter* (standard size). This equipment allows the child to manipulate while learning letter symbols and word forms. It can also be used when the child dictates a story. (Here, the child is able to see his talk appear.) The child may type his own story, science experiment, etc.

13. *Poems.* Poems can be selected for illustration, copy, or to give the child an idea for a poem of his own.

14. *Blank Books.* Blank books with pictures in sequential order may be used to let the child create his own story of a pictorial representation.

15. *Manipulative Games and Puzzles.* Manipulative games and puzzles should be available for sensory pleasure and to help with transition from real objects—to pictures, to letter and word symbols.

16. *Books and Tapes.* Teacher or children record a reading of a favorite book. Children can then listen to the recorded story.

17. *Oral Reading.* Omit embarrassment of reading in a group. Task cards might read: "Choose a story from your favorite book. Read it to a friend. Listen to your friend as he reads his favorite book." "Tape your reading. Play it back while you read silently. Can you find your mistakes?"

18. *Discarded Readers*
   a. Favorite stories from discarded readers can be taken out, illustrated and made into a *new booklet* for the story area.
   b. A booklet, composed of stories from each level of a series might be used to help *diagnose reading level*.

19. *Labels and Directions.* Labels, directions, and simple task cards in the "right" center give the nonreader a purpose for reading.

20. *Conversation.* Conversation, allowed and encouraged at work and at play, throughout the day, is a *must* for language development.

21. *Newspaper Headlines Folder.* These headlines can be used to stimulate

the child to write a newspaper article about what might have happened.

22. *Book Jackets.* Children use book jackets to get ideas for their own books, or for illustration of ideas.

23. *Surprise Bag.* A surprise bag or "Feel Box" filled with various textured objects can be used for sensory and tactile discrimination. Children feel the objects and try to guess what is in the bag. Objects should be changed frequently.

24. *Listening in Comfort.* Set up the record player with books and records on the floor with earphones. Children can sit on rugs, carpet squares, or pillows; these can be used to set the "limit" on number of children in this activity.

25. *Taping Familiar Sounds.* Use tapes and tape recorder (regular and/or casette) to allow children to tape familiar sounds. Have other children guess what they are.

26. *Filmstrips–Private Showing.* Use filmstrip projector and filmstrips for a private showing for an individual or a small group. (Show filmstrip into teacher-made screen, or place sheets of 18″ × 24″ white construction paper on back side of a divider or screen.)

27. *Super-8 Projector and Film Loops.* Film loops are close-up, colorful, and realistic. They are used best with a small group of 2–4 children, and a private showing (see 26). These are excellent to stimulate the child to observe and predict, because there is no sound accompanying the loops. Children may choose to write or record a story to go along with the loop. Keep the tapes available with the loops for other children to enjoy.

28. *Dukane Projector.* The Dukane—manual or automatic control (children like the manual)—is used with small groups (up to 6), with or without earphones. Records or tapes and filmstrips are needed materials. A *record player/filmstrip projector combination* is a good substitute for the Dukane; filmstrips with corresponding records can be used with both. (In the case of the casette Dukane, a tape recorder/filmstrip projector combination is a substitute.)

29. *Make Your Own Movie.* Film children or other action. Let the children write and plan script and produce. (If you do not have a camera, a parent might like to help.)

30. *Make Your Own Filmstrip or Slide Presentation*
    a. Of the children for "experience" feedback.
    b. Of people, places, and things unfamiliar to the children.

31. *Overhead Projector.* Make up attractive transparencies for a specific task. Use the tape recorder to go along with the activity.
    a. Use chalkboard as a screen. Children can trace over letters reflected from transparency.
    b. Transparencies of body parts might be used as guides for clay modeling.

32. *Opaque Projector.* Make up learning task cards and make them available

to the children to work with the opaque projector.

33. *Fish for Sounds*. Cut out fish, 4 inches by 6 inches. Have various sounds represented on the fish. On each fish have a paper clip that can be picked up by a magnet. Use a stick with a piece of yarn and a magnet attached to it. A child may go fishing; when he catches a fish, he may identify the sound and the letter the picture represents.

34. *A Sample Contract on Vowels*

   Name:

   Contract Skill: Vowels ā, ă, ē, ĕ, ī, ĭ, ō, ŏ, ū, ŭ,.

   Objective:

   To learn about vowels and be able to:

       a. say words having each vowel sound.

       b. identify and tell the difference in writing words with different vowel sounds.

       c. identify and tell the difference in oral words with different vowel sounds.

   Activities:

       1. I will use the records and sheets of *Listen and Do*, lessons 12, 14, 16, 18, 20.

       2. I will divide a big sheet of drawing paper into 10 parts and draw 2 pictures of each vowel sound.

       3. I will use the Language Master cards on vowels.

       4. I will play "Vowel Bingo" with a friend.

       5. I will do the red cards from the "Reading Box" that are numbered 14, 15, 16, 17, 18, and 20.

       6. I will make a "Vowel Book." On each page I will put several pictures of a different vowel sound. I will use a different vowel sound on each page.

   Evaluation:

   I will show what I have learned orally and on a written sheet during my conference with the teacher next Thursday.

(*Note*: This contract has been mutually negotiated. Therefore, activities and evaluation procedures have already been chosen. The student has been introduced to vowel sounds but is having a lot of trouble with their mastery. If he feels that he has mastered them before he completes all the activities, he has the option of renegotiating his contract and having his evaluation earlier. If he feels he does not have enough time he may wish to expand the activities and lengthen the time before evaluation. The contract is set up to last a week and a half.)

4 FINE ARTS

A Fine Arts Center should be "tantalizing" to the child's every sense. The materials should awake in him the desire to create and discover new sounds, shapes, and forms with a variety of media. This center knows no bounds, no space limitations; it is equally well expressed in the outdoors and indoors. The teacher's goal should not be concerned with the "finished product" but rather with the process by which the child receives sensory pleasure, a feeling of accomplishment, and the joy of creative expression.

ART

Environmental Resources

Storage space—cabinets, shelves, containers, baskets, and boxes should allow
the children easy access to a variety of media (it should be well organized to
encourage independence)
Clean-up equipment—buckets, sponges, and mops—should be accessible to the
children
Working space—tables, easels, countertops, floor, or outdoor space
Trays or cartons to hold paint
Aprons or substitutes—old shirts, newspaper held with clothespins, or plastic

Art Materials

Paper—a wide variety is essential; the following is a good basic list
    Construction—assorted colors for tempera painting, colored chalk (wet
        and dry), and collages. Size 9" × 12", 18" × 24".
    Newsprint—for tempera painting, crayons, charcoal, dry colored chalk.
        Size 18" × 24".
    White drawing paper—for crayons, water colors, finished paintings. Size
        18" × 24".
    Manila drawing paper—for tempera painting, chalk, water colors, char-
        coal, stenciling. Size 18" × 24".
    Fingerpaint paper—draft, butcher, frieze, or shelf (for fingerpaints or
        murals)
    Old newspapers—for chalks, water coloring, charcoal, finger and tempera
        painting, collage
    Tissue paper—for collage
    Wallpaper samples
    Cardboard
    Poster paper or tagboard of various sizes and colors
    Assorted papers of many textures and colors
    Box of paper scraps
Paste, white glue, rubber cement, wheat paste, tape, plaster of paris, instant
    papier mache
Brushes—a variety of sizes and bristle textures; most large for water color,
    tempera, paste, and rubber cement
Paint—tempera, finger, water colors (primary and others)
Clay—modeling, natural, Play Dough
Scissors—right- and left-handed
Rulers
Marking mediums—crayons, colored chalk, pastels, charcoal, pencils, magic
    markers
India ink—printing ink and stamp pad

Drawing boards, clay boards (or cafeteria trays)
Box of materials for collages
"Beautiful junk"—for creative usage and for teacher-planned activities:
        sponges, food coloring, assorted fabric scraps, string, toothpicks, wood curls and chips, yarn scraps, styrofoam packing bits, coat hangers, tubes from toilet tissue and paper towels, magazines, catalogs, newspapers, wire (chicken, florist, electrical)
Book of artists, crafts, pictures of paintings
Art prints and art objects (can be displayed anywhere)
Materials for weaving, stitchery
Drying rack or line
Paper clips, brads, staples, pins
Food coloring

Teacher-made Supplies and Tips

1. *Scissor Holders.* Holders can be easily made from gallon milk or bleach containers. Simply punch holes in the container and place scissors in holes with the points to the inside. Egg cartons turned upside down with slits in each mound also make excellent holders.
2. *Paint Containers.* Containers can range from muffin tins and plastic egg cartons to plastic soft drink cartons with baby food jars in them. These work especially well outdoors as well as indoors because they are large and not easily tipped over. Place one brush in each container; this prevents colors from getting mixed and makes clean-up easier.

3. *White Glue Containers*. Glue can be slightly watered down to go further. Good containers are those with a small tip-up pour spout, such as antibacterial soap containers.

4. *Cardboard Carpentry*

   Clay or crayon tables. Make a table of tri-wall cardboard. Cut a hole in the center of the table for a dishpan so that the dishpan will fit down in the table. Use this dishpan as a common crayon holder or for clay. The dishpan can be easily removed and washed.

   Easels. Easels to use on the floor, a table top, or outside can easily be made from tri-wall by joining two pieces together and using string on the sides to keep it upright and in an inverted "V" shape.

5. *Recipes*

   Play dough. Uncooked

       4 cups flour mixed with

       1 cup salt

       Add powder to tempera paint coloring to this mixture.

       Then add water until the mixture is soft and workable, but not sticky.

       Store in an airtight container.

   Finger paint. Liquid starch may be used in combination with powdered paint for color. Add 1 tablespoon glycerin as a preservative and store in an airtight container.

   (Glycerin. This product can be readily bought at the drugstore and makes an excellent preservative for all types of paints, such as finger and tempera. It will keep them from souring. About 1 tablespoon per unit is a good measure. It can also be used to preserve play dough.)

Some Objectives

To work with a wide variety of materials (varied sizes, shapes, and textures).

To receive sensory pleasure by working with various materials and media.

To discover color, shape, and texture by using various media.

To find success by creating an expression of self.

To use visual expression as a means of communication.

To express feelings and emotions through painting, finger painting, working with clay, and constructions.

To develop fine muscles and eye–hand coordination by cutting, pasting, painting, etc.

To introduce children to the ways great artists have expressed themselves through different media and to encourage children to do the same.

Suggested Activities

1. *Color Experimentation and Exploration*
    a. Use mixing trays containing the primary colors. Allow children to mix colors using an eyedropper.
    b. Add food coloring to water play activities.
    c. Make lemonade of the primary colors and pour together to form the secondary colors. This makes a nice snack.
    d. Make a special color concept center where children bring objects from home or make collages or paintings of a specific color.
2. *Feet Painting.* After finger painting on a roll of butcher paper, a record (with different moods) is played while children walk, tiptoe, etc., over the fresh paint. (Have pan and towels handy.) Children enjoy a pleasurable sensory experience and observe the different effects caused by the feet.
3. *Sand Painting.* Color sand with tempera solution. Apply glue to cardboard. Shake colored sand over glue design.
4. *Finger Puppets.* Finger puppets can be made to use in the home–living or block center.

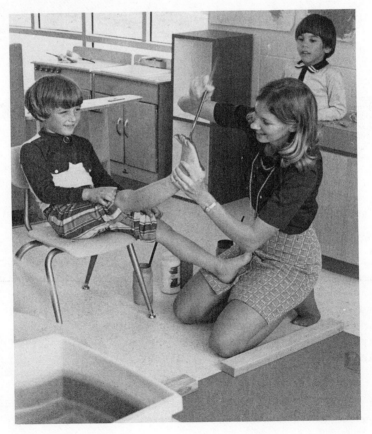

5. *Cutting and Pasting.* Children enjoy cutting and pasting from old magazines, newspapers, catalogs, construction paper, and other forms of "beautiful junk." Remember "one man's trash is another man's treasure." Keep a box in the art center for materials of this type.

6. *Designs.* Patterns of teacher-made designs can be made with tangrams, parquetry blocks, color cubes, or pieces of construction paper. Directions might read, "Can you make this pattern?" or, "Using the same materials in this design, change it and make your own."

7. *Finger-paint Prints.* Finger-paint is put directly on formica top desk or table. Children experiment with it. When they have made their finished design, finger-paint paper (shiny-side down) is placed on it, rubbed, and a print is made. (A wet sponge will get paint off the table.)

8. *Pictorial Records.* Children draw pictures of math or science activities in their work record books.

9. *Therapeutic Clay.* Place clay on boards on a table or on trays on the floor. When a child needs a vent for aggressive emotions, initiate the activity of pounding, shaping, and/or molding clay.

10. *Bookbinding.* Use cardboard of various sizes, glue, textured cloth, staples, and tape. Cloth is glued to cardboard to make hard backs for child's pictures. (Contact paper may also be used.)

11. *Block Printing.* Using pieces of bubble-type styrofoam, have children pick out designs in the styrofoam with pencils or fingers. (It is very soft and easy to do.) Proceed as in ordinary block printing. This method makes block printing possible without using sharp tools.

12. *Styrofoam Flowers.* Cut slots in styrofoam cups down to the bottom of the cup. Invert this and hold it over a hot plate. The heat will open up the strips. Do not hold the cups over the heat too long or they will melt. These flowers can be used for many things (pictures can be drawn and placed in the centers; use them to decorate Christmas trees, etc.).

13. *Coat Hanger Mobiles.* Shape hanger into a circle leaving hanger curve intact. Using yarn of different lengths, attach whatever you want to make the mobile of animals, tissue paper raindrops, members of the family the children have drawn and cut out, etc.

14. *Activity Cards.* Teacher-made cards of art ideas can be directions for a specific art activity or creative in nature, such as "What does a girafephant look like? Draw a picture or make a clay model."

15. *Art Shoebox Labs.* Labs made from shoe boxes might be added to this center. Each box has special contents and directions.

Examples:

a. Weaving. Contents: paste, scissors, multicolor strips, 8 × 10 construction paper on manila tag.
   1. Cut parallel slits in a large piece of paper in one direction.
   2. Weave strips of colored paper (over, under, over) across slits. Varying patterns can be made.

b. Wire Sculpture. Contents: wire, wire cutters, paper, pencil, wire figure. Instructions read: Draw, doodle, and experiment with pencil and paper. Copy drawing in wire.

16. *Window Finger Painting.* Children can finger paint on the inside or outside of low windows. (This improves attractiveness of room.) Windows can be easily cleaned.

MUSIC

Environment and Materials

Space
Shelves, carpet or rug
Autoharp (and cards made out with markings for familiar songs)
Kalimba (and cards made out with markings for familiar songs)
Rhythm instruments—bought and/or homemade (sticks, bells, cymbals, drums, triangles, tambourines, claves, etc.)
Zither (and cards)
Piano
Double-headed Tom Tom
Songs written on chart
Record player and records (various kinds)
Tape recorder and tapes (blank and prepared)
Earphones
Other musical instruments (guitar, uke, recorder, drum, maracas, castanets, etc.)
Zim-Gar bells (20 notes)
Manuscript paper (for children to write tunes)
Models of staff and notes, separate notes (to match and read)

Filmstrips and records correlated with music
Instruction books, charts, music books, song books
Scarves for dancing
Glasses for water, spoons
Materials for homemade instruments

Teacher-made Instruments

1. *Sandpaper Blocks.* Nail or glue sandpaper to wooden blocks.
2. *Shakers.* Fill dried gourds or two pie tins with beans and tape together.
3. *Sticks.* Use large pencils.
4. *Jingle Instrument.* Use a set of measuring spoons on a ring slapped into the hand.
5. *Drum.* Stretch cellophane paper tightly across the top of a bowl and prick with finger.
6. *Kazoo.* Use wax paper over a comb.
7. *Gong.* Old license plates (the older, the better sound they have) hit with a wad of cloth on a stick will make a gong.
8. *Jingle Bells.* Punch holes in the center of bottle caps and string on a piece of coat hanger wire to make jingle bells.
9. *Clonkers.* Hit coconut halves together.

Some Objectives

To appreciate different types of music by listening to and discussing many different styles and kinds of music.

To experiment freely with tempo, volume, quality, and sound organization by playing rhythm instruments, zither, piano, bells, or autoharp.

To use music for self-expression by body movement, singing, playing instruments, or composing songs.

To find sensory pleasure in listening to, moving, and "feeling" music.

To dramatize actions of record characters or roles of instruments.

Suggested Activities

1. *Sound Experience.* Fill glasses or bottles with various amounts of water. Experiment with tunes. Make up a tune or play one that is written out.
2. *Syllables.* Clap out "time" to names of friends.
3. *Songs.* Illustrate song written on a chart or write your own song.
4. *Expression Through a Sketch or Drawing.* Sketch or draw while listening to music. Set up paper and pencils or crayons near the record player.
5. *Listen to a Piece of Music.* After listening and discussing it, encourage an interested child or small group to write a play that depicts the action of the music; or, set up the record player and record near finger painting, painting, or clay activities.
6. *Play Music to Work By.* Music might vary from "soul" to classical.
7. *Create New Songs.* Change the words of a familiar song, create your own tune for a favorite poem, or create your own song.
8. *Word, Phrase, and Sentence Clues.* Teach songs by using the flannel board or word, phrase, and sentence chart rack. Make figures that are clues to the words of the song.
9. *Scavenger Hunt.* Send children on a musical scavenger hunt. Have them find anything they feel can make music.

10. *Write Songs.* After listening to electronic music have children write songs of their own using body sounds (clicks, claps, stamps, etc.) or mechanical sounds (keys, wood blocks, pencil bouncing on desk, etc.). Have them write songs using different phrases or repeated ones.

11. *Rhythmical "Symphony."* Prepare your own rhythmical "symphony." Write a symphony using binary from phrases AB, ternary ABA, rondo, ABACA, etc.

12. *Action Chants.* Make up rhythmical action chants such as:

A bang, a bang, a bang–bang–bang–
A slap, a slap, a slap–slap–slap.
A clap, a clap, a clap–clap–clap–
A stamp, a stamp, a stamp–stamp–stamp.

Some children chant and stamp, bang, etc., while others dance to the rhythm created.

13. *Rhythm Instrument Chants.* Make up rhythm instrument chants:

Hear the shakers go shake, shake, shake,
Hear the cymbals go ting, ting, ting,
Hear the clappers go clap, clap, clap.
(etc. . . . .)
We all go . . . (play all instruments at once)

14. *A Visiting Musician.* Invite a friend to bring an instrument, to talk about it and play it. Prepare for the visit by showing pictures and playing suitable records on preceding days.

15. *"Live" Music.* Sing cat songs while stroking a cat's fur; be a cat prowling, washing, sleeping.

16. *An Instrument File.* Collect pictures of musical instruments and music makers from colorful magazines, old textbooks, etc. Mount them and file them.

17. *Accompanying Child's Movements.* As a child (or children) runs, reels, rocks, etc., play an accompaniment on a drum, sticks, wood block, or other instrument.

18. *"Pied Piper" Effect.* Use a recorder, autoharp, piano, or another instrument when it's necessary to gather children together. Before leaving these instruments in the center, let the children talk about care of them. Set up instrument with accompanying song cards in the center.

5

HOME LIVING AND CREATIVE DRAMATICS

Role play—expressions of the self. Who will you be? The possibility is endless from Batman to a butterfly in flight. The choice is limited only by a child's imagination. This center can be a true learning experience for both teacher and child. While the child learns about social interaction, the teacher gains insight into the child's true feelings as he speaks through a "pretend" character.

Environmental Resources

Space sufficient to allow freedom of movement (close to the block center to
   allow interaction between the two centers)
Child-size furniture and appliances (table, chairs, stove, sink, bed, rocking chairs,
   cabinets, ironing board and iron, baby carriage, etc.)
Full-length mirror and hand mirrors

Home-living Supplies

Clothes for dress-up—male and female—hats, shoes, ties, pocketbooks, etc.
Play props—dishes, cooking utensils, silverware, pots and pans, etc.
Cleaning props—brooms, mops, rags, sponges, plastic pails
Telephones
Various dolls—Negro and Caucasian—baby and adult

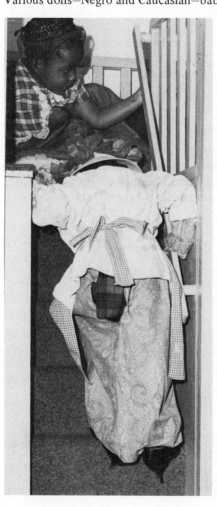

Puppetry and Dramatics Supplies

Costumes—may be the same as those for the home living or may be some which
    have a more dramatic flare
Cloth material—for creating costumes
Stage for puppets
Puppets—real and creative characters
Talk starter type cards—possibly suggesting plots for plays or for role-playing
    books, fairy tales, etc.

Teacher-made Materials

1. *Cardboard Carpentry Furniture.* Cribs or puppet stages can be made by
cutting the pieces as indicated in the illustrations.

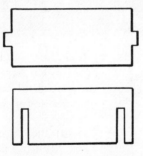

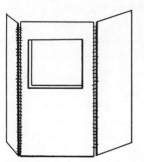

Cut stage so children on their knees can perform behind it. By joining the stage with several thicknesses
of yarn, the stage can be folded and put away when
not in use. Stage can be decorated by the children.

2. *Dolls.* Involve parents by asking them to make rag dolls for the class to use.

3. *Puppets*

   a. Large people puppets.

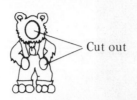

Cut out

Using a piece of cardboard as tall as the height of a child, draw a character on it. If need be, this can be easily done by using an opaque projector. Cut the figure out. Cut out a hole for the face of the child to fit in, as well as holes for the hands to go through.

   b. Stick puppets.

Either draw your own character on poster board or cut large faces from a magazine and glue them on poster board. Attach this to a dowel stick with staples.

   c. Finger puppets.

Cut holes for fingers

Cut off the finger of a glove and sew facial features on it; or trace or draw a figure approximately five inches tall. Cut it out. Cut holes in the bottom for the child to stick his fingers through. The child's fingers will be used for legs.

   d. Sock puppets.

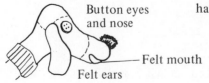

Button eyes and nose

Felt mouth

Felt ears

Sew facial features on socks and use for a hand puppet.

Some Objectives

To act out the child's world as he sees it.

To act out feelings and emotions in a comfortable setting with an accepting adult.

To find success in using the various ways one can "set up" a house, and the manners etc., used in living there.

To make puppets from various materials to use in plays and dramas.

To imitate characters from stories and films.

To provide opportunity for children to create their own stories and actions for the stories.

To practice standard American English by practicing social amenities such as using the telephone.

To interact with other children and adults in a permissive, informal situation.

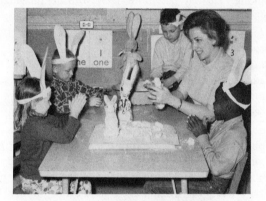

Suggested Activities

1. *Labeled Cans and Boxes*. Place cans and boxes with bold labeling on them in the center for play. These can be empty detergent boxes, milk cartons, and empty canned food containers. They should be changed frequently to keep the environment fresh and changing.
2. *For the Reticent Child*. Encourage the reticent child to use a puppet for talking. He may talk more freely with the imaginary character than he will with the teacher.
3. *Live Flowers*. Cut live flowers to use in the center to give it a warmer atmosphere.
4. *Washing Clothes*. A washtub and clothesline on an adjoining outside area add zest to this center. Allow the children to use the tub to wash the clothes they play with in the center.
5. *New Products*. Change the center often by bringing new products to use in the kitchen or new hats to suggest different roles. Save what you take out of the center and return it at a later date.
6. *Playhouse*. A large refrigerator box with doors and windows cut out makes an exciting place to play. Let the children paint or decorate it as they wish. (This can make a good office, library, barbershop, etc.)
7. *Complete Change*. The center can be completely changed to resemble a special period of time, or a special place, such as another country.
8. *Special Activities*. To make the center lively and exciting, add these materials:
   a. *A post office*—A counter top of a book case or window (or a puppet stage), stamps, play money, letters, telephone, postcards.
      Mailboxes can be placed in several other areas in the room for pick-up and delivery.
   b. *A store*—A counter, cash register, play or real money, labeled boxes and cans, a price marker, newspaper ads, advertising bargains a telephone for receiving orders, and shopping carts.
   c. *A beauty and/or barbershop*—Full-length mirror (turned on its side) on a long table, combs, brushes, wigs, play razor, shaving cream, makeup, rollers, clips, pins, play shampoo, dryer, uniforms, capes.
   d. *Election booth*—Refrigerator box, paper ballots, names of candidates, curtain, official, voters.
   e. *A public library*—Shelves, books, divider for quiet area, stamp for dates, cards. This is a good place to share books the children themselves have written and illustrated.

SEWING AND COOKING

Extended Activities

Although these areas are by their very nature ones that require fairly close supervision, this should not discourage you. By participating in them, children learn many things about measurement and increase their realm of experience. A primary consideration for both of these activities is simplicity. While children enjoy sewing and cooking, they can tire of waiting too long to participate, to see, or to enjoy the finished product. Because these activities excite children a great deal, it is necessary that they be exceptionally well planned. Think carefully about the materials needed, especially with cooking, because many of the materials that are used are not common to the classroom. Invite parents to come and direct or participate in the activities.

Sewing Equipment and Supplies

Sewing machine (if possible)
Fabrics—various textures and shapes
Needles—small and large (these should have eyes large enough for the children to thread themselves, or have needle threaders handy), knitting, crochet, embroidery
Thread and yarn of all colors
Scissors (sharp enough to cut materials)
Embroidery hoops, designed cloth
Pins, buttons, beads, thimble
Burlap
Trays for sewing materials
Pattern on a chart—put up simple directions and pictures to explain the steps

Cooking Equipment and Supplies

Measuring spoons and cups
Minute timer
Variety of mixing bowls (preferably with a handle)
Hot plate (or a stove if you are lucky and your recipe calls for baking)
Saucepans—variety of sizes
Wooden spoons and spatulas
Eggbeater
Paring knives
Cookie cutters of aluminum (preferably with handles or knobs)
Pot holders
Aprons
Dishpans
Rolling pins

Chart—Using a sentence chart you can put up pictorial recipes or worded recipes. This lets you know what has gone into the mixture and helps the children remember too.

(Recipes may call for other items, but this gives the class a good general supply.)

Recipe task cards—Laminated cards such as the following may be used by individual or several groups of children.

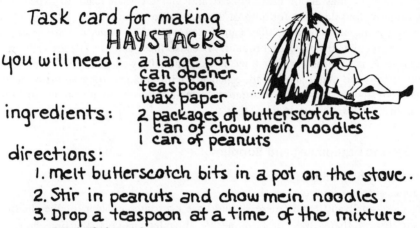

Task card for making
HAYSTACKS

you will need: a large pot
can opener
teaspoon
wax paper

ingredients: 2 packages of butterscotch bits
1 can of chow mein noodles
1 can of peanuts

directions:
1. melt butterscotch bits in a pot on the stove.
2. Stir in peanuts and chow mein noodles.
3. Drop a teaspoon at a time of the mixture on wax paper.
4. Cool.
5. Eat.

★ Remember - the careful cooks leave the center clean for the next cooks.

Some Objectives

To discuss, plan, and share work with others.

To learn quantitive measurement by experimenting with all forms of measuring—liquid, dry, length, width, etc.

To read pictorial and/or written directions.

To enjoy the experience of creating a product.

To cook and taste different kinds of foods.

To interact with adults as well as other children.

SEWING

Suggested Activities

1. *Pillows.* Make simple rectangular pillows for the children to use when resting.
2. *Patterns.* Draw simple patterns for doll dresses or puppet bodies. Let the children cut out the material and sew the clothes.
3. *Stringing.* Stringing is a good beginning activity. String popcorn for a Christmas tree, or bits of styrofoam for a necklace.
4. *Creative Stitchery.* Maintain a scrap box of material for creative stitchery.

5. *Burlap.* Draw pictures, letters, names, or designs on burlap; outline them in yarn.

6. *Raveling.* Ravel the edges of rectangles, squares, or circles of burlap. Stitch around the edges to prevent further raveling. These could be used in the classroom for doilies, or as place mats in the center.

7. *Sewing Cards.* Make your own sewing cards for the children to use. Use a simple outline picture or design with holes to sew through; use numbers and make a dot-to-dot sewing card.

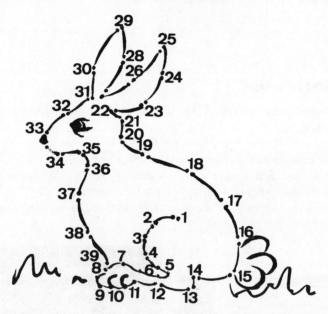

8. *Cloth Book.* Have the children make books out of cloth. They can sew the backs together and make yarn pictures in them.

9. *Sewing Kit* (*Shoebox Labs*). A brightly colored shoe box might contain a sewing kit with a simple pattern, scissors, thread, needles, pins, material, and instructions. The instructions might say: "Pin pattern to double thickness of material. Cut out and then stitch together."

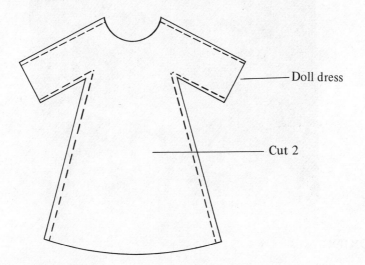

Doll dress

Cut 2

10. *Sewing Game* (*Shoebox Lab*)

Contents:	Set of cards with a pattern of numbered dots, needle and thread
Instructions:	"Pick a card. Thread a needle. Tie a knot at one end of the thread. Follow the dots." (*Note*: Any angle can be used as a pattern. Sew from one dot to the opposite dot the farthest away.)

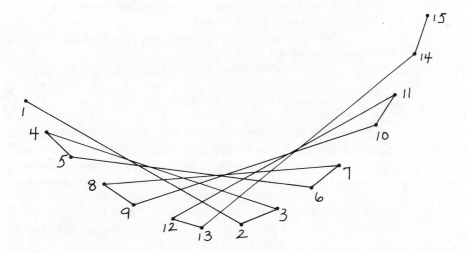

COOKING

Recipes and Activities

Every ingredient that goes into cooking is edible, so let the children taste them all.

1. *Jello.* This is a good beginning recipe. Be sure that a refrigerator is available. (Often the one in the cafeteria can be used.)

2. *Popcorn.* Equipment and ingredients:

   A large pot, hot plate or popcorn popper (a popcorn popper can be used for many different cooking experiences)

   Popcorn, oil and butter, salt

   Measuring cup and spoons, bowls, and charted recipe

3. *Applesauce.* Equipment and ingredients:

   Apples, plastic serated knives (these are sharp enough, yet are safe)

   A pot, water, sugar, hot plate

   Let the children peel and cut up apples. Put the apples in a pot with enough water to start them cooking. Cook until tender. Mash. Add sugar (1 cup per 6 apples); cook for 10 more minutes. Add cinnamon if desired. Cool and serve. Delicious for snack with milk.

4. *Banana Milk Shake.* Mash a ripe banana in a bowl. Pour 1 cup milk over the banana. Beat with an eggbeater. Fill 2 glasses with milk shake.

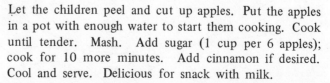

5. *Girl Salad*

Face: Canned peach half, round side up

Eyes: Raisins

Nose: Clove

Mouth: Cut from maraschino cherry

Collar: Stand half ring of pineapple on edge

Dress: Hide a canned pear half under a lettuce leaf shirt and let pear show for the petticoat

Slippers: Tuck cherry halves under the petticoat

6. *Boy Salad*

Face: Canned pear half, using same material for features as girl

Hair: Shredded carrots, or grated cheese

Trousers: Half a canned peach cut straight at the sides with a notch at the bottom in center

Legs and arms: Pineapple wedges

Buttons and pocket trim: Cut from maraschino cherries

7. *Peanut Butter Cookies* (*no bake*)

Ingredients: eggs, peanut butter, butter, vanilla, salt, confectioners' sugar, peanuts

Recipe: Beat until smooth: 1 egg, 1/3 cup peanut butter, 1 tablespoon soft butter, 1/2 teaspoon vanilla, 1/8 teaspoon salt, 1 cup confectioners' sugar.

Gradually add 1 more cup confectioners' sugar.

Shape into tiny balls.

Roll each ball in 3/4 cup finely chopped peanuts; refrigerate.

8. *Peanut-Cocoa Cookies*

Ingredients: 1/4 cup cocoa, 2 3/4 cups sugar, 1/2 cup butter or margarine, 1/2 cup milk, 1/2 cup peanut butter, 3 cups quick-cooking oatmeal, 1 teaspoon vanilla

Recipe: Mix together sugar, butter, cocoa, and milk. Add peanut butter, oatmeal, and vanilla.

Cook about 2 minutes after mixture begins to boil. Drop spoonsful on wax paper and let cool.

9. *Gingerbread Man*

Ingredients: 1/2 cup butter or margarine, 1 cup sugar, 1 egg, 1 1/2 cups flour, 1 teaspoon baking powder, 1 teaspoon ginger

Recipe: Cream butter and sugar together. Add egg. Mix in flour, baking powder, and ginger.

Roll out this dough. Cut out shape of man.

Bake at 375° until brown. Try making other shapes too.

10. *Circus Cookies*

Ingredients: confectioners' sugar, vanilla, milk, vanilla wafers, animal crackers

Recipe: For icing wafers—

Mix together 2 cups confectioners' sugar, 1/2 cup milk, 1 teaspoon vanilla.

Spread this mixture between the vanilla wafers to make a sandwich cookie. Place a dab of icing on top of the sandwich. Stand an animal cracker on each sandwich.

11. *Gazpacho*

Ingredients: 1 cup chopped tomato, 1/2 cup green pepper, 1/2 cup celery, 1/2 cup cucumber, 1/4 cup green onion, 2 teaspoons parsley, 1 small clove garlic, 1/2 table-spoon olive oil, 1 teaspoon salt, 1/4 teaspoon black pepper, 1/2 teaspoon Worchestershire sauce, 2 cups tomato juice

Recipe: Chop all vegetables, crush garlic clove, combine all ingredients, chill overnight.

Enjoy. (This is a good follow-up recipe after a trip to the market or a unit on foods.)

12. *Tacos*

Ingredients: 2 lbs. ground beef, 2 tomatoes, 2 onions, 1/2 lb. cheese, ketchup, can of prepared hot dog chili, taco shells

Recipe: Brown ground beef; add chili.

Shred and grate the vegetables and cheese.

Place all of these in the taco shell.

Top with ketchup.

(This activity is a little more advanced, but it is a very good one to follow a unit of study on Mexico.)

13. *French Toast*

Ingredients: 2 eggs, 1/2 cup milk, 1/4 teaspoon salt, 6 slices slightly dry bread, syrup, jelly, and butter

Recipe: Beat eggs, milk, and salt. Cut bread in half slices. Heat a heavy skillet.

Dip bread in batter. Saute in 2 tablespoons of butter.

Brown on both sides.

Add more butter as needed.

Serve hot; top with jelly and/or syrup and butter.

14. *Snow Balls*

Ingredients: 2 cups crunchy peanut butter, 3/4 cup marshmallow
cream, 1/2 6-oz. bag chocolate chips, shredded
coconut

Recipe: Blend all ingredients and form into 1-inch balls; roll in
shredded coconut; refrigerate if too soft to handle.
(The coconut may be dyed in different colors if desired
for seasonal emphasis. Balls may also be rolled in
chocolate sprinkles or other cake decorations.)

15. *Energy Cookies*

Ingredients: 4 cups uncooked rolled oats, 3 cups unbleached
white flour, 2 cups dates (pitted and chopped),
6 tablespoons milk, 1 cup brown sugar, 1 1/2 cup
corn or peanut oil, 1/2 cup maple syrup

Recipe: In large bowl beat together sugar and oil. Add oats,
syrup, flour, and milk. Mix in dates.

Preheat oven to 350°. Oil cookie sheets, roll dough into
small balls, and flatten them on cookie sheets.

Bake for 15 to 20 minutes. Let cool. Makes 60 cookies.

16. *Apricot Coconut Balls*

Ingredients: 1 1/2 cups ground dried apricots, 2 cups shredded
coconut, 2/3 cup condensed milk, confectioners'
sugar

Recipe: Combine apricots and coconut. Add milk. Mix well.
Shape into 1-inch balls, and roll in sugar. Place on waxed
paper to dry for one hour.

17. *Breakfast Nook*

Place toaster, bread, butter, jelly, and butter knives on a table in
home-living center. Allow a few children at a time to have breakfast. This is especially good for some children who do not get
breakfast before they come to school. Ask the parents to help
you with the upkeep. A powdered fruit juice could also be added
or make your own fresh.

INVESTIGATION
IN SCIENCE
AND MATHEMATICS

The young child will refuse to limit his investigations and study of nature to any center. A ladybug that crawls, a rock that sparkles, an ant carrying bread on its back, an opening flower, a spider web, a drop of dew are mysteries that excite the curiosity of young children. These are the types of experiences that should be encouraged in the young child, for these and countless other "moments of learning" are the ways in which young children discover the nature of materials and form concepts in science and math.

Environmental Resources

Rugs
Tables
Low shelving for puzzles, games, displays
Windows (preferably low enough for the children to see out)
Clear plastic containers with labels for "raw materials"
A small plot of land (left in its natural state, if possible)

Science Supplies

Prisms, tuning forks, wood, wire, glass, soil, bottles, candles, batteries
Bolts, switches, pulleys, levers, screws, wheels and axles, planes and pendulums
Pendulum frame, pendulum bobs, scales (balance, kitchen, spring), weights
Assorted materials for balancing, blocks of various weights, mirrors, lenses
Kaleidoscopes, electric bell, calendars, clocks, hour glass, egg timer, sundial
Bulbs, tape measures, yardstick, meter stick, rulers, dry and liquid measure
    containers ,
Rope, drinking straws, food coloring, stopwatch, stethoscope, sponges, keys
Kite, locks, iron filings, magnets, mechanical junk, slinky
An assortment of chemicals from home: vinegar, baking soda, table salt, baking
    powder, sugar, cream of tartar, rubbing alcohol, epsom salts, iodine, ammonia,
    and hydrogen peroxide
Fibers—nylon, silk, rayon, linen
Magnifying glasses (hand, and large on stand), compass, barometer, flashlight
Objects to smell, taste, touch; gears, strings, color paddles, telescope
Microscopes
Heat, water

Math Supplies

Dominoes, (large and/or small), flannel sets and flannel board

Magnetic letters and numbers, magnetic board, fractional parts and fractional board

Playing cards, checkers and board, chess set and board

Rope (for encompassing areas), puzzles, logs, counting pegs and boards

Blocks of all shapes and sizes, number blocks, parquetry blocks

Sum stick, adding machine, play money, colored beads, math games, flash cards

Trundle wheel, compass, measuring rods and containers, geoboards, Cuisenaire rods

Number line, abacus, collections of all types (buttons, coins, stones, sticks, stirrers, macaroni, beans, yarn, marbles, bottle caps)

Egg cartons for making sets

Books—interest and reference

Catalogs, newspaper ads

Teacher-made Materials

1. *Find the Place Value.* Using tagboard, fasteners, and beans, children can use this game to find the place value and record it.

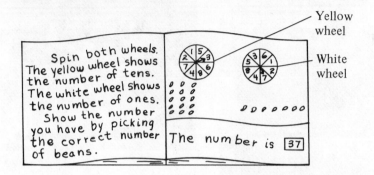

2. *Tic-Tac-Toe.* Use laminated tagboard for all parts of the game (plain board, problem cards, X's and O's). Turn cards face down. Students may take turns taking top card and answering the problem (answers are placed on back of cards for self-correcting). One student takes X's, another takes O's. When a student answers the card correctly he may put X in any square he wishes to try to get three in a row, just as in pencil tic-tac-toe.

3. *Pitch-a-Penny.* A penny is thrown and lands on a square or section. That number is the score. Add points together or subtract whenever penny lands on that square. The first person to reach a score of 100 wins. This may be made with laminated tagboard, tri-wall, or regular cardboard.

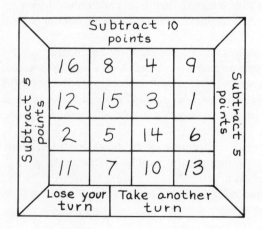

4. *Math Drag.* Use colored tagboard and laminate. One to four children may play the game. Each throws the dice, moves that number of spaces with his car, and adds or subtracts the number within the space he lands on to remain there. The first student's car to reach the end of the drag strip wins.

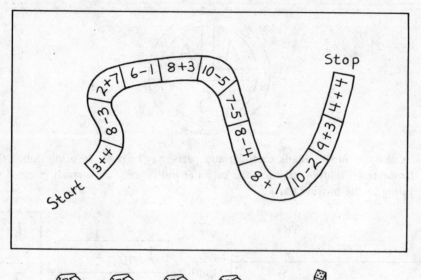

5. *Addition Wheels.* Use colored tagboard and laminate. Wheels may be painted on both sides for self-correcting. Clothespins may be used to clip on correct number.

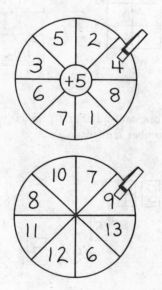

6. *Sectioned Paper Plates*. In the two smallest sections of this plate, draw an A to represent addend. Draw an S in the largest section to represent sum. Pegs or other types of counters may be used. The children place the counters in the A section and then determine the sum.

7. *Calendar Game*. Blank calendar and parts may be made by using tagboard; laminate. Children may use the calendar individually or in small groups by filling in the missing parts.

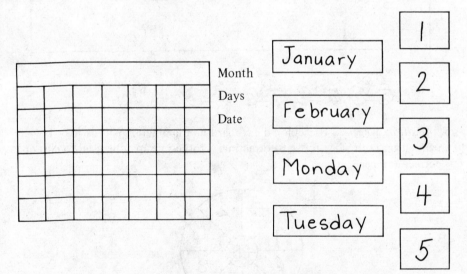

8. *Number Dogs*. Cut dog and numbers from tagboard; laminate. Children can put together for number sequence.

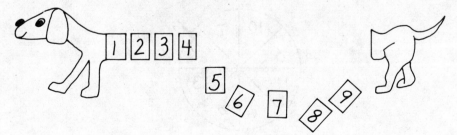

9. *Counting Cards.* Using a rectangular tagboard card, write the numeral 5 (for example). Make five small squares near the bottom of the card. Use clothespins to cover each of the little squares. On the back of the card, place the number word, five.

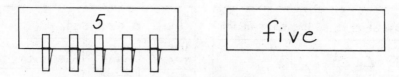

10. *Clothes Hanger Counters.* Staple a number card on the neck of a clothes hanger. Clip on clothespins to represent the number shown on the card. This may be used to teach number stories or for drill on missing addends by using two colors for clothespins.

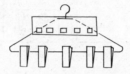

11. *Rubber Dice Cubes.* Using an electric carving knife, cut foam rubber squares. Use a permanent magic marker to number the cubes 1–6 or 4–9. Children may use them as dice; they may roll these dice and add the numbers or subtract from the larger number; they may be color–coded for learning place value; they may be used to learn "less than" and "greater than."

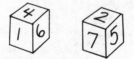

12. *Number Trains.* An engine and a caboose are drawn with intermediate cards 1–100. Students may use these task cards asking to: "Make a train with cars 1–10"; "Make a train with cars numbered 68–75"; "Make a train with two cars whose numbers add up to 12"; "Make a train with three cars whose numbers add up to 20."

13. *Math Card Box.* Various math skill cards may be color-coded according to difficulty. Most skill cards have a corresponding answer card that can be found by a number and the color coding. A few are of the sort that an answer sheet is not appropriate. This is indicated on the card by a symbol.

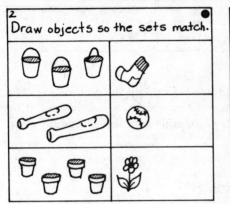

14. *Spool Game.* Using six tinker toys and sticks, a student may roll dice and try to get all rolls 1–6 and therefore spools 1–6. Skills involve counting dots on dice and recognition of numbers 1–6.

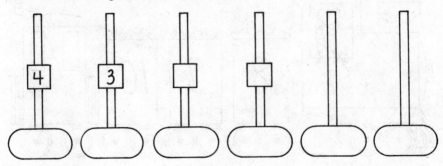

15. *Bottle Cap Game.* A board, three bottle caps for each player, and the score pad will be needed. The board may be made from contact-covered cardboard and six-pack plastic divider. Students stand behind a line and toss caps; after three turns the scores are added up.

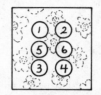

16. *Number Feet.* Using tagboard, twenty or more feet can be made, each containing a number, numeral, and like set. Laminate for durability. Students may put feet in numerical order and then walk in them or they may rearrange them for adding and subtracting.

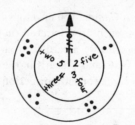

17. *Wheel Turn.* Three wheels, each one larger than the other, and placed on top of each other, may be made by using tagboard and then laminating. The wheel contains numbers, the numerals, and the sets. A student must line up each wheel to match (*examples*: 3, three, [:·]).

18. *Math War.* This may be played with cards made with laminated tagboard and each card containing a subtraction or addition fact. All cards are given out; each student turns over his top card and then subtracts or adds the numbers on the cards. The student with the highest answer takes both cards. Answers are placed on back of each card for self-correcting.

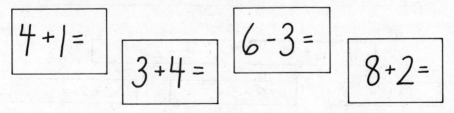

19. *Pegboard Counting.* Two pegboards, used with golf tees—one showing counting in ascending order and the other in descending order—are needed for this activity. The student may place the corresponding number of golf tees beside the appropriate number.

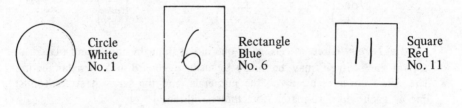

20. *Beanbag Toss.* Using twelve or more different laminated tagboard shapes, each different also in color and with a number from 1—12, the student or a small group of students may place them on the floor. The student throws a beanbag and should name the number, color, and shape the beanbag lands on.

Circle
White
No. 1

Rectangle
Blue
No. 6

Square
Red
No. 11

21. *Addition and Subtraction Game.* Ten envelopes or library card holders with numbers from 1 to 10 on each are mounted on a board such as a materials bolt board. A child may choose a card from a pile containing a variety of addition and subtraction facts and place it in the correct pocket (answers are placed on the back of the cards for self correction).

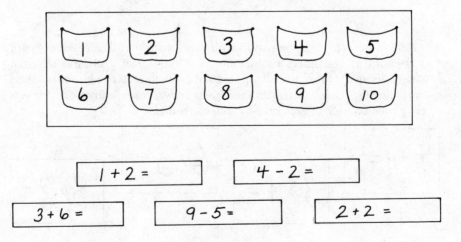

22. *Match the Sets Bingo.* This game can be played like regular bingo or independently. A student must match each set on his card with the set that is
shown on the cards that are drawn. The sets are matched by contents and the
number in the set.

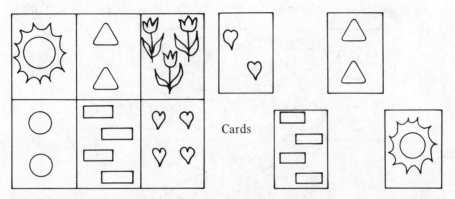

Cards

23. *Feel It Sorting Game.* Laminated tagboard cards of different shapes are
made with a variety of different textured materials glued on top of each.
Students may put on blindfolds and then sort according to shape and texture.

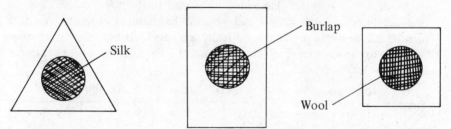

Silk

Burlap

Wool

24. *Counter Box.* A colorful box containing cans filled with different counters
(bottle tops, different-colored small sponges, dyed macaroni, straws, colored
sticks, corks, buttons, colored spoons) may be placed in the math center to
help students needing concrete materials.

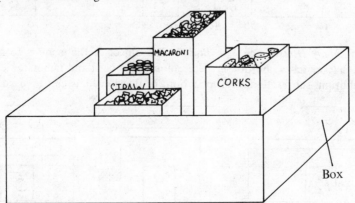

Box

25. *Take a Chance—Add or Subtract.*   Two or more children may play this game using an egg carton with a number in the bottom of each section and two dice. Each student shakes the egg carton with the dice inside; dice will land on two numbers. The student can either add or subtract the numbers; each correct answer is worth 1 point. The first to reach a score of 20 wins.

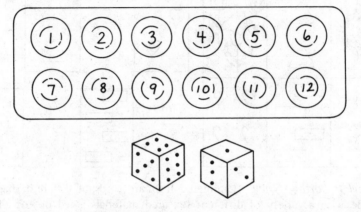

26. *Addition and Subtraction Football.*   The game board or "football field" can be made with cardboard, laminated tagboard, or a window shade. Two or more children spin the spinner and advance that number of spaces. Yardage can be gained if the problem is correctly answered. If not, the player must go back to the spot from which he advanced. The first person to get to the goal line wins.

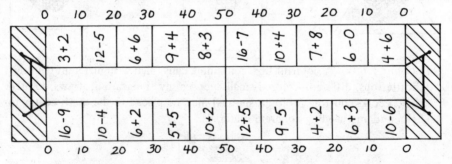

27. *How Many Houses Can You Build?*   The object of the game is to find the roof that matches the house. Use colored tagboard and laminate; a variety of addition, subtraction, multiplication, or division facts can be used.

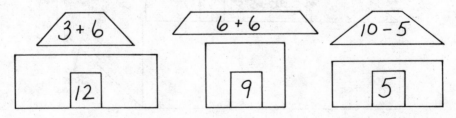

28. *Turn a Card*. Turn a pile of laminated cards containing addition and subtraction facts face down. Students may take turns drawing cards and solving problems; the cards may be placed on the correct answer. If desired, a score may be kept by adding the answers to the cards.

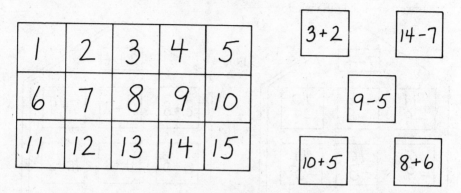

29. *Addo*. Using a variety of addo and problem cards made with tagboard and laminated, a small group of students may play this game just the same as bingo.

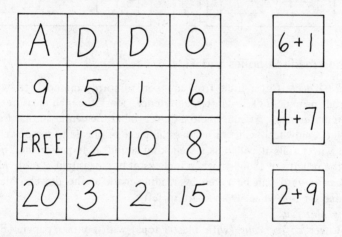

30. *Magic Numbers*. Using poster board or tagboard, cut large rectangle cards; put a number on each card; laminate; and cut into four pieces. When pieces are put together a number appears. These may be stored in brown sturdy envelopes.

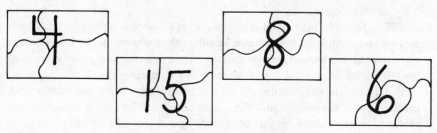

31. *Number Houses*. Using colored tagboard, make several houses with windows, each window containing a number fact. Windows open to show correct answers. Laminate before cutting windows. Children slip papers inside house and open windows to write answers. Slide papers out and check. The answers are inside the windows.

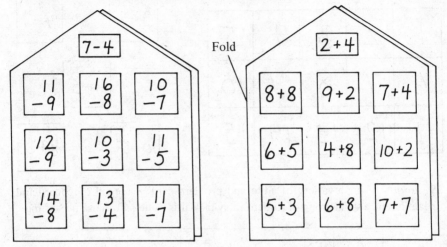

Teacher-made Supplies and Tips

1. *Trundle Wheel*. Cut a circle from any sort of sturdy material (tri-wall, thin plywood, or paneling) 36″ in circumference. Mark the inch measures around the circumference. Attach this to a dowel rod at the center so that the wheel spins like a pinwheel. Glue or nail a small piece of plastic to the dowel so that as the wheel rolls it will make a clicking sound as it passes the 36″ mark. Start the roll at the 1″ mark; when it clicks, it has measured 1 yard. Measures less than a yard can be taken by reading mark at the dowel. Mark inch measures on the wheel from right to left.

2. *Sorting Material*
   a. Cover *coffee cans* (with plastic tops) with contact paper. Fill each container with a different kind of bean or macaroni. Even acorns or large seeds make good materials. Children can use these for sorting sets or for weaving and measuring.
   b. Collect *styrofoam trays* (meat or vegetable) and use for sorting colors, shapes, objects, etc.

3. *Smelling Jars*. In baby food jars, place a small piece of sponge. Soak each piece of sponge in different common liquids with strong smells, such as alcohol, ammonia, cloves extract, lemon extract. Have the children guess what they are. By using baby food jars, the scents can be preserved.

4. *Task Cards*. Develop "things to do and investigate" math and science task cards to pique the child's curiosity. Some cards will be simply questions and pictures, while others might be sample games for the children to play.

5. *Color Paddles*. Using the primary colors, cut out cellophane circles. Glue these into separate circular frames of tagboard. These can be used to learn about the formation of secondary colors from the primary.

6. *Balance Scale*. Balance scales are easily built, but the sturdier the materials you begin with, the longer they last. By making the baskets different colors, children will have an easier time expressing which basket needs more or less to balance.

7. *Tangram*. A tangram (Chinese puzzle) can be made from a square (of any size) colored tagboard or cardboard, then cut into seven pieces. Bisect the square diagonally. Bisect one of the large triangles. Take the other triangle and use 1/4 of the longest side as the side dimension of the square and short side of parallelogram. Cut out carefully. (These can also be cut from tile or linoleum, using a knife as a cutting tool.)

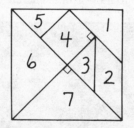

8. *Tangram Cards*. Combine some or all of the tangram pieces to make unique designs. Trace the outside line of these on tagboard to make tangram cards. Geometrical shapes on tagboard make simple cards.

9. *Geoboards*. Geoboards can be made for or by the children. Use a plywood square and 100 nails (10 rows with 10 nails each). Children can use these with colored rubber bands to make designs while discovering shapes and angles.

Some Objectives

To discover basic math and science concepts by exploration and experimentation (in incidental and contrived situations).

To use a variety of materials for weighing and measuring.

To chart progress and results of experiences.

To use the scientific method of problem solving—to observe, identify problem, predict, research, test prediction, and generalize.

To develop habits of thinking and investigation.

To use resource materials in problem solving.

To enjoy science and math activities by engaging in various methods of discovery.

To share discovery with others.

To find success in these areas.

To manipulate various objects to move from concrete experiences to the abstract.

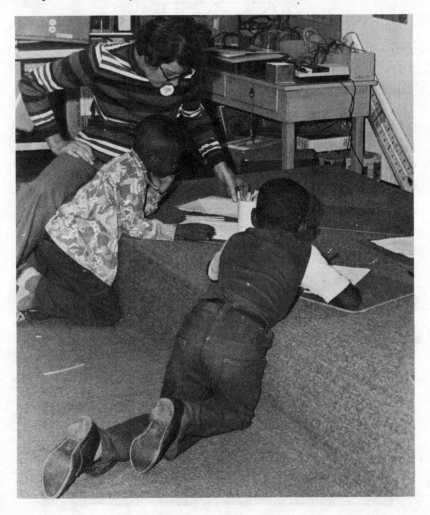

Suggested Activities

1. *Task Cards*. In various areas of the center, directions or suggestions might be given via learning task cards (written or pictorial). Wording for some cards might read: "Weigh your shoe." "Can you repeat this design using new colors?" "Mr. Number Man—Can you find an 8? Add his shoelace and his ears."

2. *Cards for Outside* might read: "How many times will the trundle wheel turn between the school and the gym? Record your findings."
3. *Number Line*. Use oilcloth and magic markers or tagboard to make a large number line on the floor for children to walk on.
4. *Ropes and Tile*. Place a rope on tile. "How many blocks are inside the rope? How many are partially inside the rope? Can you solve it by addition? by multiplication?"

5. *Calendar.* Make the daily calendar one that can be done without supervision. Include many different parts. It might be placed at the same location as a board the children use daily to turn their names and denote their presence.

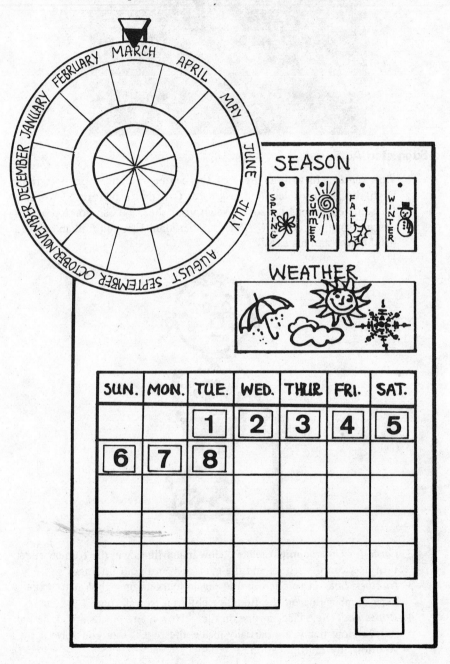

6. *Weather Observation.* On a large chart, keep a weekly record of the weather.

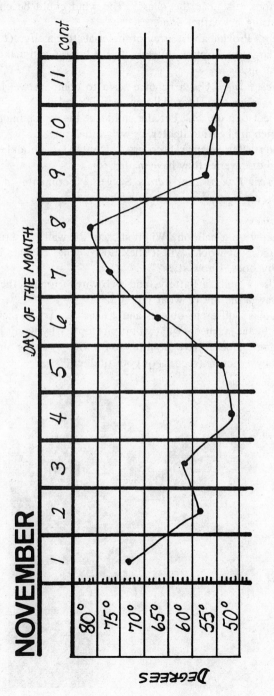

7. *Charting Temperature*. Chart temperature on a graph. Some of the older children can do this with the observation of some younger. Place thermometers near the chart. The wind could be charted the same way using a weather vane.

8. *Sorting*. Provide a vast array of materials to classify. (*Examples*: hard/soft, large/small, plastic/metal, etc.) Children can make their own classifications.

9. *Balance Scale*. Use a balance scale to compare weights and sizes of various objects. Have children record results.

 Select one object. Let the child sort the remaining things according to which are heavier, lighter, or weigh the same.

10. *Booklet*: "My Science Discovery." Display large booklet for individuals to add discoveries they have made.

11. *Discovery Box of Task Cards*. Suggest experiments in a discovery box of task cards.

 Examples:
 a. "Blow up a balloon. Will it stick to the wall? Try rubbing it against a piece of wool. Will it stick now? What changes have happened? Why does it now stick?"
 b. "Use a bulb, a battery, and two wires to make the light come on. Draw a picture of what you did."
 c. "Collect different objects and a magnet. Try to pick up the objects with the magnet. What will it pick up? Why won't it pick up everything? Does it have anything to do with what the object is made of? Draw a picture (record) of your findings."

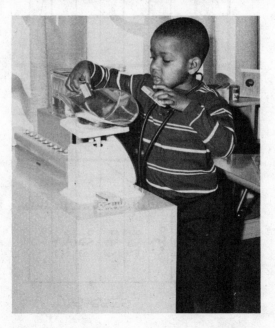

12. *Time.* Allow time for the child to have free exploration: to look, feel, weigh, measure, test, and predict on his own. Observation might occupy most of the young child's time spent in this center.

13. *Supermarket Ads, Catalogs.* Use ads or catalogs for on-the-spot shopping. A folder might read: "You have $25.00 to spend. What would you buy? List items and prices and place the list in the folder. You might use the adding machine to check your totals."

14. *Shoebox Lab.* Cover a shoebox with contact paper or paint and shellac to make a beautiful lab with independent activities:

Example:

Magnets: Box contents might include magnets, a box of iron filings, various metal objects and nonmetal objects. Instructions on the box: (1) What happens with 2 magnets? (2) Move iron filings by placing magnet under box. (3) Which objects cannot be picked up with a magnet?

ENVIRONMENTAL EXPLORATION

Materials and Supplies

Low shelves for display
Table for display and usage
Washable cover for table
Empty containers and jars for children's contributions
Aquarium and terrarium (empty)
Flowers and plants; animals—alive and preserved
Rocks and shells
Cages and animal food
Paper and pen for labeling
Chart and graph paper
Resource material, pleasurable nature reading (*Example*: *Rick Ranger*)
Watering can, trowel, seeds, flowerpots, magnifying glass, microscope, incubators,
    thermometers, bug house (to keep live insects)
.Field microscope

Teacher-made Materials

1. *Match-by-Land, Water, and Air*. Using three pieces of colored tagboard, tape
   them together with pictures on each one to depict land, water, and air. Several
   pictures representative of each can be mounted on cards. Children can match
   each picture with the appropriate land, water, and air. Answers can be placed
   on back of each card for self correcting.

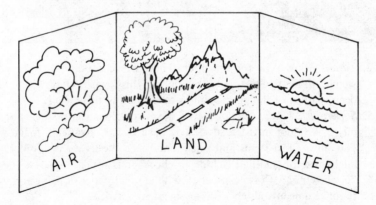

Cards

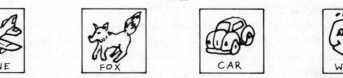

2. *Seed Identification*. The chart can be made by using tri-wall, cardboard, or tagboard. A sample of each kind of seed with the word under it may be put in the chart. Several additional seeds of the same varieties are placed in a box labeled seeds. Children can find seeds that match and paste them on the chart. Others may desire to do research on the various kinds of seeds.

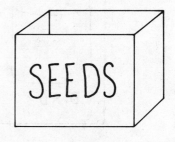

3. *Animals and Their Homes*. These puzzle parts may be made with wood, cardboard, or laminated tagboard. One piece of each puzzle has a picture of an animal; the matching part has a picture of the animal's home. Words may be added if desired and answers placed on the back for self-correcting.

4. *Eco-Cycle Circle*. A dish or circle containing words of the elements necessary for animals and plants to live can be made with laminated tagboard. Sets of picture cards to match the words can be made using the same materials. One odd card can be made; the player who plays the odd card on the cycle wins the game.

5. *Bird*, *Animal*, *or Fish*. Three envelopes or library card holders (each one labeled either bird, animal, or fish) may be mounted on a board (cardboard, laminated tagboard, or material board). An individual or small group of children can pick picture and word cards from a deck and sort them in the representative pockets. Names are on the back for self-correcting.

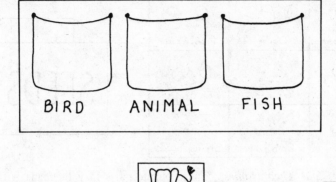

6. *The Date Game*. Using tri-wall, cardboard, laminated tagboard, or material board, mount three pockets made with envelopes or library card holders. Label the four pockets: Day, Month, Holiday, Season. Make several picture and/or word cards; an individual or small group of children can sort them into the pockets accordingly. Label the back of the cards for self-correction.

Some Objectives

To find out about natural things by observing, exploring, and investigating.
To handle live animals.
To plant, to keep animals and plants alive, to classify and label animate and inanimate objects, to build an aquarium.
To develop a positive attitude toward living things and their interrelationships.

Suggested Activities

1. *An Aquarium. Note*: Because movement and changes are so easily viewed in the water, an aquarium is perhaps more attractive to children than growing plants. This is excellent for understanding concepts of interrelationships—between plants and animals.
   Materials needed:
   A glass aquarium
   A layer of soil for water plants to root
   A layer of sand to keep the soil down
   Stones and shells for creatures to rest on and hide behind
   Pond water, if available. (Tap water often needs to be filtered.)
   Inhabitants—select creatures that live together harmoniously. Children might like to research to find which ones do.
   Plenty of space
   Snails are important, for they act as scavengers
   Food for the inhabitants (be careful not to overfeed)
   Pond weed (necessary both for food and to keep the tank clean)

   If desired: filter pump, charcoal, filter fiber
2. *Earthworm Farm*
   Materials needed:
   A fairly wide and deep jar or an old aquarium (filled within 4–5 inches from the top)
   Add: A layer of small stones
        Layers of soil of various colors (sand, gravel, dark soil, etc.), well pressed down
        A layer of living turf
   Stick a narrow strip of paper down the outside, marked to show where the layers are.
   Completely cover from bright light (with cloth or black construction paper) or place in a dark place to accelerate burrowing. Keep covered when you are not watching the worms.
   The children can:
   Put the earthworms into the farm.
   Observe the disturbances in the earth made by the worms.
   Give them fresh food daily (lettuce, cereal, cornmeal).
   Add moisture to the soil frequently.
   Go in the schoolyard and look for animals living in the soil.

3. *Displays of Live Weeds and Wild Flowers*

   Note: These are excellent for helping children understand the concept of diversity. Comparative studies such as:

   a. Comparison of weeds found at the school with those found near the pond or creek.

   b. Comparison of wild flowers found on a slope facing the sun with those found on a slope not facing the sun.

   c. Comparison of weeds found at school in the country with those found by a friend in the city (in sidewalk cracks) will give children an idea of the diversity of plants found around them and their relationship to the climate, etc.

   Example:

   Display a beautiful weed. (*Example*: dandelion or horseweed.) Direction card or a great deal of discussion might evolve around: "Why Is This Plant Called a Weed?"

   Collections and classification should be done by children with the assistance of resource materials and the teacher.

4. *Observation–Measurement–Charting*. Observe the growth of seeds or plants in the room (height, new leaf or bloom). Record observations. Measure leaf spread and/or stem growth. Record growth.

5. *Small Garden* (for the nature center). This is a substitute where outdoor gardening is unfeasible. Gardens aid the child's understanding of the concept of change. (*Note*: With a little direction, the children can make such a garden for themselves.)
Materials needed:
A plastic or metal dishpan can be used although the ideal is a zinc-lined box with a hole for drainage.
A soil mixture. (The children will help mix the soils and probably question why.)

When the layout is ready, it should be discussed with interested children. They will offer suggestions. Research (and the teacher) will let them know what is possible in such small gardens. The children should decide on some workable plan, which should be accepted.
Suggestions.
a. *A sunken pond* (made with a dish), with the garden planned around it. Even a small pond will hold a few tadpoles, a snail, and some pond weed.
b. *A rockery* (made from snail rocks collected by the children) can be made by placing soil between the rocks in which plants take root. Tiny rock plants can be bought cheaply at dime stores and nurseries or may be donated by the parents.
c. *A lawn can be sown.* Here children can plant different varieties of grass seed.
6. *Vivarium* (a home for such creatures as frogs, toads, and salamanders, that live on both land and water).
Materials needed:
A screened wooden box
Soil to partially fill box
Shallow dish to serve as a pond

7. *Ant farm* (for scientific observation and watching division of labor).
8. *Animals and Appropriate Cages*—gerbils, mice, rabbits, chicken, snakes, etc.
    (Learning to love and care for pets helps a child to develop a positive attitude toward living creatures.)
9. *Displays for Children's Contributions*—caterpillars, spiders, ladybugs, sprouting onion or potato, moulded bread, falling leaves, rocks, sea shells.
    (*Children should be encouraged to preserve life at all times.* Do not let them destroy for the sake of collections.)
10. *Outdoor Gardening*
    Materials needed:
    Tools (child–size)—hoes, rakes, shovels, watering cans, hose, spade, trowels
    Land with good soil and sunlight or flower boxes
    Thermometers
    Wheelbarrows
    Seeds, bulbs, and plants
11. *Plant Identical Seeds or Plants.* Use different types of soil, amounts of sunlight or water. Compare each group.
12. *Outdoor Exploration and Field Trips.* These are extremely necessary to encourage and stimulate the young child's natural curiosity about nature.
    Suggestions:
    a. *Walks* (around and about the school, with or without the teacher). The child should be encouraged to look slowly and carefully. He might observe: changes of the leaves, nests made by birds and squirrels, sounds made by animals, creatures hiding under stumps, logs, or rocks, a running brook, a mud puddle, a clump of weeds, spider's eggs, the first flower to bloom, a ripening strawberry, erosion of soil, a budding tree, depending upon the location of the school and the season.
    b. *Pond or stream collections.* (When exploring these areas, children might use a plankton net to collect microscopic animals to observe with their field microscope or to return to the classroom to observe with the microscope.)
    c. *Visits to and exploration of river banks, quarries, or salt marshes* (dependent upon location), *a mountain stream*, etc.
    d. *Utilization of state parks.* Their resource people can be utilized as guides for wildlife study and their museums can be used for reference.
    e. *"Star parties"* held at night for those children and parents who are interested in viewing the stars (with or without a telescope) and the planets (if a telescope is available).
    f. *Campouts in local parks*, etc. (with planned nature walks and time for free discoveries). It is important that the teacher have a "positive" attitude toward this experience, for it will permeate to the children.

13. *Examining Seeds.* Cut open fruits and vegetables with the children. Examine the different kinds of seeds: sizes, shape, number, color, etc. Label with a marker in clear sandwich bags; match seeds to fruits and vegetables; match seeds to picture or drawings of fruits and vegetables. Plant some of the seeds.

14. *A Sample Contract on Seeds*

    Name:

    Objectives:

    1. To find out and be able to show or tell how plants produce their own kind through seeds.
    2. To find out and be able to show or tell three ways that seeds travel.
    3. To find out and be able to show or tell the four parts of a seed.
    4. To learn about and be able to tell the difference in six kinds of seeds.
    5. To learn that we eat some seeds and be able to show or tell about four kinds of seeds that we eat.

    Resources:

    Books: *Carrot Seed* by Ruth Kraus
    The Little Seed That Grew by Sara G. Klein
    Where Do Seeds Come From? by John Carey
    My Petunias by Betsy Smith
    Filmstrips: *How Green Plants Grow*
    Seeds Grow Into Plants
    New Plants from Seeds
    Plant Experiments

    Activities:

    1. Take a walk and find all the seeds you can.
    2. Try to find or draw pictures of different seeds. Make a book of them and write the names of the seeds.
    3. Make a seed book. Paste different seeds on the pages and write the names of the seeds.
    4. Plant a bean seed in a cup of dirt and watch it grow.
    5. Cut open different fruits and look at the different seeds.
    6. Find some pinecones and look for their seeds.
    7. Put the pinecone in a bowl of water and see how the pinecone protects its seeds.
    8. Soak bean seeds overnight. Pull the bean apart and describe what is inside.
    9. Put a bean seed in a small jar with wet cotton. Watch and draw what happens to the seed for two weeks.
    10. Look outside for some seeds. Then figure out how they traveled.
    11. Play the "Seed Game" matching the seed with a picture of the plant it comes from.

12. Sort seeds from the big box in an egg carton.
13. Use an encyclopedia or a science book to find out what kinds of seeds we eat.
14. Make a shoe box movie theater that shows how a seed grows into a plant.

Reporting:
1. Show your collection of seeds and tell about it.
2. Pretend you are a seed and show three ways you could travel.
3. Show your plant and tell us what you did to make it grow.
4. Pass around your "Seed Book."
5. Make a mural to show what happens when a seed is in a sunny, moist place.
6. Write a story about what kind of seed you would like to be and why.
7. Make a picture out of seeds.
8. Pretend you are a seed and write a diary about what happens to you every day for two weeks.

15. *A Sample Contract on Baby Animals*
Name:
Objective:
   To learn to match the parents and babies by sorting pictures of different kinds of animals.
Activity:
   Use the animal picture cards and put each family into an envelope. You may use the book *True Book of Animal Babies* and the film *Finding Out How Animal Babies Grow*.

Objective:
   To learn to read the names of fifteen different animals by making puzzles.
Activity:
   Find pictures of fifteen different animals in magazines. Paste them on the left side of a strip of poster board and write the name of the animal on the right side. Cut the board in the middle and make a puzzle. Work your puzzles.

Objective:
   To learn how a tadpole turns into a frog and keep a record of it.
Activity:
   Find some tadpoles in a nearby creek. Bring them to school and take care of them. Each day write a sentence and draw a picture of the way the tadpole looks.

Objective:

To find out how we can best care for pets by learning what they need to live and giving an oral report on the findings.

Activity:

See the filmstrip *Care of Pets*. Write down the main things pets need to live. Tell the class about it.

Objective:

To learn how animals move differently by observation and then to teach several students different ways animals move.

Activity:

Go to the zoo and draw pictures of four different ways animals move. Lead the class in singing and acting the record, *Sammy*, which sings about the different ways animals move.

Objective:

To find out how weather changes the ways animals live and illustrate this.

Activities:

Read the books *Mrs. Goose's Thanksgiving Party*, *All Ready for Winter*, and any others you might find. Make a mural that shows the differences in the life of a bear in spring, summer, winter, and fall.

7

MOVEMENT

Through the movement education approach, the child learns just what his body can do in all kinds of situations and relationships. Immediate involvement is the usual response as the child seeks to solve the problem in movement. The child need not fear that there is a wrong answer to a movement problem.

Environmental Resources

Open area

Record player and records

Tambourine or drum for signaling and setting rhythmic tempo

Climbing apparatus (indoor and outdoor). This might be improvised indoors with sawhorses.

Other apparatus—low horizontal ladder and other free-form climbing structures are highly desirable for the playground in addition to tire swings, items for "obstacle courses," sewer pipes set in concrete, rubber tires, steps, and climbing ropes. (See Chapter 8.)

Per 3–5 children:

Mat—4' × 6'

Balance board—2' × 4' may be used

Per child:

Ball—various sizes, 6"–8"

Rope—7'–8' of #10 sash cord with ends taped to prevent fraying

Beanbag

Plastic hoop

Wand—20"–24" long

Can—2 lb. coffee tin with plastic lid

Shuttlecock—outdoor plastic badminton bird

Assorted rhythm instruments

Suggestions to the Teacher

1. Discuss with the children and agree on a signal to be used when it is time to stop and listen.
2. State the problem or challenge briefly, in direct terms.
3. When a piece of equipment is involved, indicate what the child is to do as soon as he gets his equipment. Immediate involvement is preferable to waiting until each child has his rope, ball, or beanbag before beginning the activity.
4. Remind the children to avoid collision with one another when they are working in the general or shared space. This requires constant attention and good body control. It is, therefore, a better learning condition than having the children always move in the same direction.
5. Encourage children to wear comfortable clothing that does not bind or impede free movement of any body part. Barefoot participation is highly recommended if the floor surface is splinter-free. The muscles of the feet work more efficiently, and tactile sensation is enhanced with walking barefoot.
6. Avoid demonstrating the movement in order to prevent preconceived notions about the solution. Once the children are involved, good examples of the solution to the problem by various children can be pointed out to the class with the suggestion that others might want to

try that particular solution to the problem. It should be made clear that such examples represent another way of responding, not the right way to respond.

7. Allow time for practice and creativity. Free choice of any activity for a given time will allow the teacher to observe and suggest individual problems to be solved. Encourage children to make up games to be played with the equipment or games involving the apparatus. They are thereby made responsible for stating the problem or challenge.

8. Praise and reinforce the child's efforts to explore the limits of his motor ability. Challenge him to create new ways to solve the problems you give him.

Some Objectives

To explore and discover the motor abilities of the body.
To develop body control.
To develop fine and large muscles of the body.
To seek out relationships of the body with the space around it.
To find delight in free body movement.
To improve problem-solving individually and jointly with others.

Suggested Activities

I. *Where the Body Moves*

    A. *Space.* Personal space is that space occupied by the individual which does not infringe on the space of another. Shared or general space is the space the group as a whole uses.

       1. Explore your own space:

          a. How tall is it? How wide is your space?

          b. If you keep one foot still and move the other, can you make your space wider?

          c. Touch as much of your space as you can at one time. Can you do this at a high level? A low level?

          d. See how little of your space you can fill at one time.

       2. Explore the shared space:

          a. Can you travel about the room, moving quickly, without touching anyone? Try it again and change directions each time you hear the signal (a whistle, drum, or tambourine tap).

          b. How would you move if all our space were filled with cotton balls. Show me how you would move the cotton balls with different parts of your body.

          c. Can you travel about the room staying very close to one another without touching? How would this look in slow motion? How would you move if you were late to school?

    B. *Direction* (forward, backward, sideward, diagonally, up, down)

       1. In your own space:

          a. Can you move your arms in different directions? In front of you? Sideward? Behind you? How about your feet?

          b. Who can stretch one arm in one direction and the opposite leg in another direction? (This assumes that the concept of "opposite" has been learned.) Can you change your level and do it another way?

2. In the shared space:
    a. Can you change directions each time you hear the signal?
    b. Who can hop in more than one direction?
    c. Can you walk, change directions, and still face the same direction? Can you walk backward to your space without touching anyone?
    d. Find a partner. See if you and your partner can both move in the same direction when the tambourine rattles and in different directions on the taps of the tambourine. (Indicate the different sounds from the tambourine so the class recognizes the two signals; establish a firm rhythmic beat.) Try this with music and small groups of three or four. Allow brief time for practice and then share each group's "directional pattern" with the class.

C. *Level.*
    1. In your own space:
        a. Put yourself at the lowest level possible in your space. Can you move two body parts at this level? Can you move your whole body at this level?
        b. Is it possible to have your head lower than your feet? Is there another way?
        c. Show me how you can keep two different body parts low and one body part high.
    2. In the shared space:
        a. Begin your run at one level and end your run at a different level. Can you think of another way?
        b. What level is best for stopping at the end of a run? What level is best for a quick change of direction? (Encourage experimentation with the idea of lowering the body level with a wide stance in order to stop or turn.)
        c. Can you travel, changing your level and direction on the signal?

D. *Pathways* (straight, curved, twisted, zigzag)
1. Can you move forward with a pathway that is *not* straight? Show me a different way.
2. Who can move like a corkscrew?
3. How would you move if you were an arrow shot from a bow? (The "why" of this movement could correlate with a science lesson.)
4. Can you and a partner make a zigzag pathway with your ropes? A twisted or curved pathway? Can you combine these pathways and hop along them?

II. *How the Body Moves*
A. *Time* (fast, medium, sudden, sustained)
1. Can you be a machine that begins very slowly and then moves faster and faster? Repeat with a change of level.
2. When you are ready, travel very quickly until you hear the signal, then stop. Repeat, but on signal, stop and slowly change your level on 4 drumbeats (or tambourine taps). Can you show me a different level this time?

B. *Force* (strong, light)
1. How would you travel if you were pushing a heavy box? Pulling a loaded wagon?
2. Can you walk like a giant? Run like a deer?
3. While the music plays, change from heavy, strong movements to light ones each time you hear the signal (drumbeat, whistle, tambourine tap).

C. *Flow* (bound, free, combination of movement)
   1. Can you balance at one level and then change to another level, very smoothly? Let's try to balance on 4 counts (drumbeats) and change levels on 4 counts. Ready? Begin: "balance," two, three, four; "change," two, three, four.
   2. Travel as the music plays, "freeze" when it stops. (Discuss the meaning of "freeze" if the children fail to stop quickly.)
   3. Who can jump, roll on the floor, and end in a stretched position? (Caution the children to land softly, bending the knees as they lower themselves for the roll.) Try this again moving as smoothly as possible.
D. *Tensed–Relaxed*
   1. Can you show me what happens to a popsicle in the sunshine? Be a cup of water that changes to an ice cube.
   2. Can you slowly tighten all your muscles as the drum beats 4 counts and relax 4 counts? This time show me a change of body shape (curled, twisted, stretched) as you tighten. Are you able to change your level as you relax?
   3. Can you tighten all at once on one drumbeat and relax on 3 counts? Can you slowly tense on 3 beats and relax completely on one drumbeat? (Encourage changes in levels and body shapes.)
   4. Move like an iron man and then like a rag doll when you hear the signal. (Try this to music, letting the children alternate their movements at will. Praise any sense of rhythmic pattern exhibited.)
E. *Relationships* (near–far, alongside, in front–behind, over–under, leading–following, unison–contrast)
   1. Can you place yourself over your wand (beanbag, jump rope)? Alongside it? Under it? Behind?
   2. On the signal, can you move as far as possible from your spot and then return to your spot on the second signal? Change the level or the force of your movement this time.
   3. Be very still and listen to the music. Then let some part of your body move to the music; let the movement grow bigger until it takes you all over the room. Repeat with a different body part leading.
   4. "Mirror" your partner's movements when the tambourine rattles and try to contrast your movements with his on taps of the tambourine. (Precede this challenge with a discussion of what it means to mirror and contrast movements. Examples of contrast: fast–slow, up–down, strong–light, and so on. May be done to music.)
III. *What the Body Does*
   A. *Body Shape* (stretch, curled, twisted, wide, narrow, tall, short)
      1. Show me a tall, twisted shape. A curled shape at a low level. A wide, stretched shape.
      2. Is it possible to curl one body part and stretch another? Can you twist one part and curl another?

3. Let me see you stretch, then twist, then curl your body. Show me a different way as you change your level. Can you make three different body shapes as you travel about the room?

B. *Parts of Body* (leading, supporting, transferring, receiving, initiating)

1. Show me how many ways you can move your head, your arms, your feet and legs, your trunk. This can be done to music as the children combine different body parts in movement in personal space or as they travel about the shared space.

2. Find a way to make a bridge, supporting your weight on three body parts. Who can show me another way?

3. Can you support your weight on one body part and shift your support to two body parts with a smooth movement?

4. What is a good way to land after you jump or leap? Why? (Stress the best way to absorb force: by giving with the force, i.e., bending in the hips, knees, and ankle joints when landing.) What is a good way to catch a ball that is moving very fast? Why? ("Give," as if pulling the ball into your midsection.)

5. Who can jump off the end of the balance beam, land softly, curl, and roll? (Mats are needed. *Hint*: roll on the rounded parts of your body.)

6. How would you toss your beanbag, catch it, and go into a roll on the floor?

C. *Locomotor Movements* (to run, walk, crawl, roll, hop, skip, jump, leap, climb, slide, gallop, push, pull, etc.)

1. When you are ready, move about the room as quickly and quietly as possible, changing directions on the signal. Remember not to touch anyone.

2. Can you jump from one foot and land on two? Can you jump backward?

3. Who can skip at a high level? Can you skip backward? (Progression for "nonskippers": hop two times on the right foot, lifting the left knee high; hop two times on the left foot, lifting the right knee high. As child becomes proficient, alternate one hop right, one hop left, emphasizing lifting opposite knee high each time. This is the basis for skipping.)

4. Let me see you travel about the room at a low level, changing your way of moving on the signal. (Crawling to rolling, to running, to giant steps, and so on.)

5. Get together in groups of three and arrange the equipment so you have to use as many different kinds of movement as possible. (Give each group a rope, a balance beam, or box from which to jump, and a mat. The children are to arrange an obstacle course that requires rolling, crawling, jumping, walking zigzag, and so on.)

6. Find a partner. How many ways can you move your partner: pull, push, roll your partner? (Point out examples of good body mechanics, i.e., getting down low and close to one's partner in order to apply force for pushing or rolling; lining up one's body in the direction of applied force in pulling.)

D. *Nonlocomotor Movements* (to swing, sway, twist, turn, curl, stretch)
   1. Can you swing one body part and then another? Can you swing your whole body? Can you swing with a partner? (Try this with music and/or rhythmic accompaniment.)
   2. With a partner can you make a very twisted shape? A combined high and low stretched shape?
   3. As you sway back and forth or from side to side, can you show me different body shapes (curled, stretched, twisted, and so on).

Copyright, 1972, *The Courier Journal* and *Times*. Reprinted with permission.

E. *Manipulative Movements* (to throw, catch, strike, kick)
1. Balls
   a. How many ways can you move your ball?
   b. Can you travel and move your ball at the same time? (Walk, toss, and catch; run, tap ball with feet, and so on.)
   c. Can you and a partner move the ball from one to the other with good control? What helps you control the movement of the ball?
   d. Bounce or pass the ball to any person who does not have a ball; keep balls moving all over the room. (Use as many balls as the group can control.)
2. Beanbags
   a. What body parts can you use to move your beanbag?
   b. Toss and then catch your beanbag with a different body part—other than your hands.
   c. Can you toss your beanbag so it lands in front, behind, beside you?
   d. Can you toss your beanbag and clap once (twice, three times) before you catch it?

3. Ropes
   a. How many ways can you move over your rope? What ways can you travel from one end of your rope to the other? Can you move backward along your rope?
   b. Can you jump over your rope while turning it? Can you jump while turning your rope backward?
   c. Can you travel about the room while you turn and jump your rope?
   d. What ways can four of you work with one rope? With two ropes?
4. Hoops
   a. Show me different ways to move around the outside of your hoop. Around the inside.
   b. Can you stretch as you move into your hoop and curl and roll as you move out of your hoop?
   c. Who can twirl the hoop around some body part? Show me a different way.
   d. How many ways can you move through the hoop as your partner holds it? Can you move through a rolling hoop?

5. Wands
   a. As you hold the wand with both hands, can you step forward and then backward over the wand?
   b. Can you stand the wand in front of you, turn quickly, and catch the wand before it hits the floor?
   c. Can you balance the wand on your hand or finger? Can you move forward and backward or sit down as you balance the wand?
   d. Can you and a partner have a tug-of-war holding the wand? Can you do it at a different level?
6. Large tin cans
   a. Show me a statue as you stand on one foot atop your tin can.
   b. Move about the room quickly, traveling around or over all the cans without touching them or another person.
   c. Can you toss your shuttlecock and let it bounce off the lid of the tin can when it comes down?
   d. Can you toss your shuttle and then catch it in your tin can? (Remove plastic lid.)

7. Balance boards
   a. How can you move from one end of the board to the other with good balance?
   b. Can you walk halfway across, then balance, leaning forward with arms held out to the side and the other foot held high in back? (*Hint*: Look straight ahead, not down.)
   c. Who can walk halfway across, stop and then change direction to finish?
   d. As you move across the board, show me two balanced positions before you finish. (Balance is aided by a wide base of support and/or a position which is lower to the floor.)

IV. *Rhythmic Activities*

  A. *Individual Work*

   1. Sit comfortably on the floor, close your eyes, and listen to the music. Can you move just your head in time to the music? Now move your head in one direction, pause, and then in another direction, pause, and so on. (Stress the "pause" as being a positive element rather than merely an absence of movement. Such rhythmic pauses are either the logical ending for a movement or the preparation for a new movement. This concept of pauses or stillness as being a positive element is basic to confident rhythmic response; it indicates purpose and control.)

   2. Show me how many ways your hands and arms can move in response to the music. Now your feet. Can your movements lead you as you dance around the room? How about your feet?

   3. Stand like a floppy rag doll and listen to the drum. Can you start a movement in your trunk that takes you all about the room? (Vary the rhythm of the drumbeat and stress pauses that end a movement or begin a new one.)

   4. Choose a rhythm instrument and when you are ready, play a rhythm for yourself as you dance around the room. This time, see if you can change your level and pathway as you move. (Pathways can be curved, straight, twisted, zigzag.)

   5. As you move, can you make a different body shape each time you hear a different sound? (Shapes—curled, stretched, twisted, tall, short, narrow, wide. Vary sounds—drum, bell, maracas, claves, tambourine, vocal sounds.)

   6. Ask the children to suggest various words that describe or depict movement—creeping, dashing, springing, balancing, rising, sinking, growing, flowing, and so on. Make a list of these words and ask each child to choose one or two of them as a theme for his dance. Rhythm instruments or body percussion can provide accompaniment. If the children feel secure, have them share their dances and let the class guess which words served as themes for each dance.

  B. *Partner Work*

   1. Face your partner and do a "mirror dance" with your hands and arms. Can you do a mirror dance with feet and legs?

   2. Hold hands with your partner and skip (slide, leap, gallop) until you hear the signal, then find a new partner and continue to move to the music.

   3. Move the same way your partner moves until you hear the tambourine; then move in a different way. (Encourage contrasting movements as well as strong unison movement. This challenge can be either locomotor or nonlocomotor.)

   4. What interesting body shapes can you and your partner make? Can the two of you create an interesting design in the space you share? Practice until you two can make three different designs with various

body shapes and levels; then let's do these designs to music. (The concept of purposeful pause is basic in this problem as the children finish one design and prepare for the next, holding the final design longer to give a strong ending to their dance.)

C. *Group Work*

1. On the signal can you move toward the center of the room and away from the center when you hear the signal again? (*Hint*: Remember not to bump anyone. Recorded music may be used for this. Allow time for controlled movement in the center, occasionally, before sounding the signal to move away from the center.)

2. Be seated in groups of four. Each child does a mirror arm dance with the child sitting opposite to him.

3. All children seated in a circle on the floor. Take turns leading a rhythmic pattern with body percussion. Can you work out a rhythmic pattern to your name and share it with the group?

4. Assign each small group (3 to 4 children) a movement theme and let them make up a short dance. Suggested themes: "Grow and stretch as flowers do, opening their petals." "Be leprechauns creeping out for a frolic in the moonlight." "Be calm ocean waves which become rough and tossed by a storm." The theme from a favorite story or poem may be chosen. The dances may be accompanied or unaccompanied. Remind the children of elements which make movement interesting—change and contrast in direction, level, strength, tempo, pathways, body shapes, and relationships in movement.

8

OUTDOOR PLAY

Life is an adventure of sunshine, imagination, and freedom in the child's world of outdoor play. The spaces, surfaces, and equipment should create an environment for learning. These are the media through which children can develop physical strength, motor coordination, dramatic play, creative activities, and social skills.

Environmental Area

150 square feet of play area per child
Variety of topographical features: mounds, flat, sod and turf, pine needles, and sand
Balance of space in the sun and shade
Hard-surfaced area for wheel toys and bouncing balls
Grassy plot for running and romping
Spot for pets, garden, and digging
Sandpit and cover (with brick or concrete surroundings for a place to sit)
Space for water play
Storage space for equipment
Safety precautions
Natural areas with a variety of plant life: trees, shrubs, grass, weeds, flowers
Outdoor weatherproof electrical outlets

Stationary Equipment

Interesting structures or sculptures for climbing
Swings (tire or leather seats)
Platforms for climbing and/or swinging
Large sewer pipes set in concrete
Equipment for crawling and tunneling
Tree trunks
Low horizontal ladders
Low climbing ropes
Wading pool

Copyright, 1972, *The Courier-Journal* and *Times*.
Reprinted with permission.

Portable Equipment

Walking boards—various lengths
Sawhorses—various heights
Wooden steps, wooden ladder
Heavy wooden benches
Low balance beams
Bales of straw
Tires (tractor, automobile, bicycle)
Balls
Beanbags
Jump ropes—long and individual
Transportation equipment: wagons, tricycles, wheelbarrow, go-carts, broom-
  stick with sock head
Sand toys
Tools for gardening: shovels, rakes, hoes, etc.
Building blocks
Tools for woodwork
Scrap lumber for large construction
Wooden boxes, packing crates, rope handles, cardboard cartons
Planks
Steering wheel and column attached to a heavy box

Copyright, 1972, *The Courier Journal* and *Times*.
Reprinted with permission.

Parent–made Equipment and Materials

1. Storage unit to build:

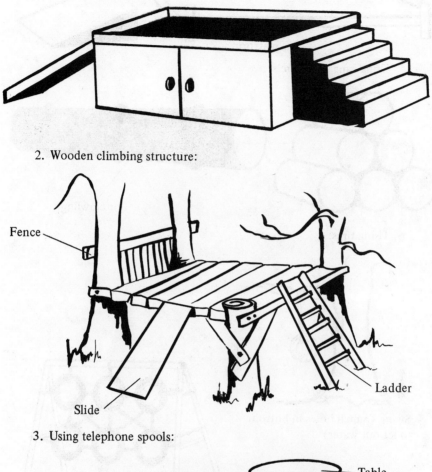

2. Wooden climbing structure:

Fence

Slide

Ladder

3. Using telephone spools:

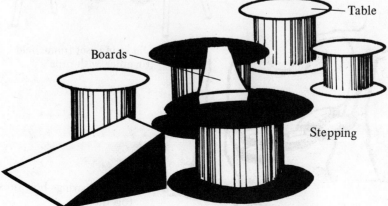

Table

Boards

Stepping

4. Wooden bridges and structures:

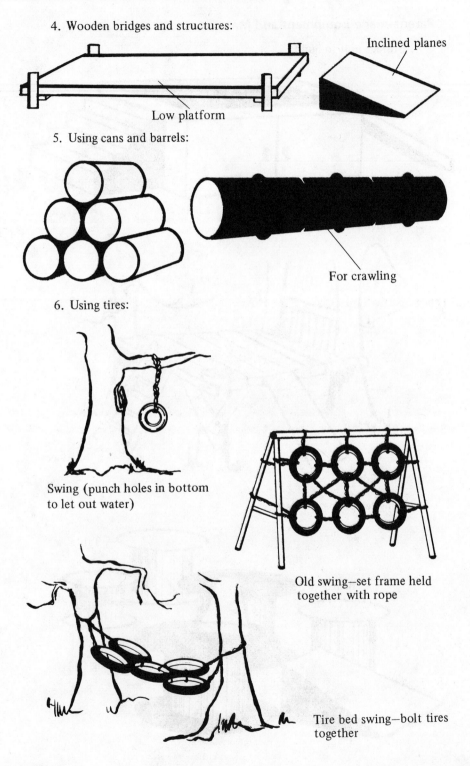

Inclined planes

Low platform

5. Using cans and barrels:

For crawling

6. Using tires:

Swing (punch holes in bottom
to let out water)

Old swing—set frame held
together with rope

Tire bed swing—bolt tires
together

7. Rolling slide:

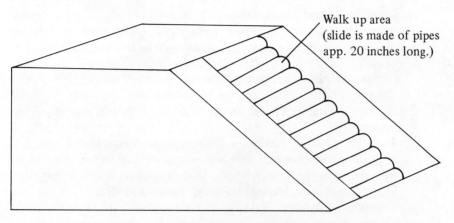

Walk up area
(slide is made of pipes
app. 20 inches long.)

8. Trees encircled with brick: (May be used as a quiet area for small group
   teaching, storytelling, or dramatic play.)

9. Nets for climbing:

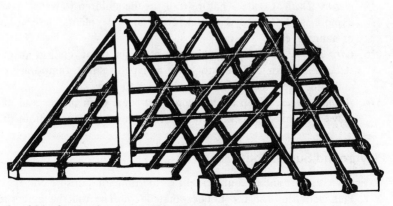

Rope should be knotted at intersections

Suggested Activities

1. *Spontaneous and Directed Play.* Structure the outdoor environment so that the child will have many opportunities for spontaneous, creative play as well as directed play. Children should be free to engage in either or both.

2. *Hopscotch.* Paint a hopscotch square on an asphalt area.

3. *Obstacle Course.* Plan an obstacle course requiring such things as crawling through pipes, stepping through tires, climbing, crawling under bars, etc.

4. *Movement Courses.* Instigate active movement courses such as "Station one, gallop like a horse; station two, leap like a frog; station three, bend like a tree in the breeze, etc." Include walking, running, jumping, hopping, galloping, leaping, skipping, climbing, dodging.

5. *Extension of Indoors.* Take out as many indoor activities as possible—painting, blocks, dolls, etc.

6. *Task Cards.* Make task cards of possible games the children might enjoy. Remember to make the wording as simple as possible.

7. *Change Equipment.* Create interesting situations for climbing, crawling, etc., by changing the equipment frequently.

8. *Jump Rope.* Use the jump rope on the ground to create geometric designs and shapes; have the children "walk" the shape.

9. *Large Bag of Rags.* For emotional release, hang a large bag of rags from a tree and use it as a punching bag.

10. *Tussles.* When tussles occur on the playground, allow the children to fight it out—in slow motion.

11. *Rope Net.* Hang a rope net between two trees (good for swinging or climbing).

12. *Exercising.* When they are exercising, ask children to suggest an exercise and let them lead it.

13. *Playhouse Change.* From time to time, place an interesting playhouse on the playground, such as a camping tent or teepee.

14. *Nature Trail.* Create a nature trail for the children to walk through, to explore, and to enjoy. (Creek, trees, animals, plants, natural habitats of animals, etc.)

15. *Carpentry.* Keep tools, wood scraps, nails, paint, etc., in an outdoor storage area for children to build and paint small, temporary objects and structures. Adult assistance is advised here.

16. *Animal Cages.* Keep animals and cages near both indoor and outdoor play environment for children to observe and enjoy throughout the day.

Playground Suggestions

1. Give support and encouragement to the timid and unsure child.
2. Plan activities for the uncoordinated child so that he may succeed.
3. Be patient with all types of children in their endeavors.

4. Make the playground an interesting learning situation by adding art, music, reading, science, and other activities.
5. Slides need top platforms. Slides built into hills and mounds are safest.
6. Swings should be out of heavy traffic areas.
7. Sawdust or sand should be placed under all climbing apparatus.
8. Place trash cans on the playground.

9 PEOPLE AND PLACES: THE SOCIAL STUDIES

Coping in today's world becomes increasingly difficult for each generation due to the rapidity with which our American social order is changing. How does a child five to eight years old cope, or learn to cope? By being faced with experiences that challenge him to feel—to feel as an individual and as a member of a larger community. By dealing with and experiencing different "people and places" the child is made more aware of his niche in today's society.

Environmental Resources

Table and 4–6 chairs
Bulletin board
Storage space
Community resources—people, places, things

Materials

Activity kits (*Example*: Community Helpers)
Globe and maps
Reference books
Blocks, transportation toys
Typewriter
Language master and cards
Tape recorder and tapes
Dukane—filmstrips, tapes or records
Animal cages
Paper—writing, construction, chart
Clothing for dramatic/role play
Objects from other cultures—flags, costumes, coins, pictures, etc.
Materials for career awareness centers
SVE study prints

Teacher-made Materials

1. *Slide Down the Community Slide.* Use colored tagboard and laminate.

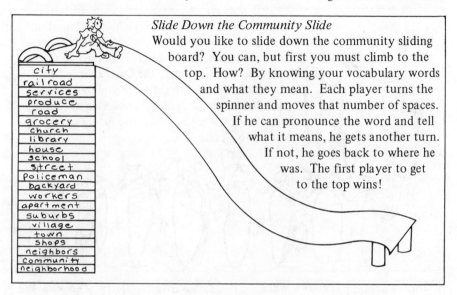

city
railroad
services
produce
road
grocery
church
library
house
school
street
policeman
backyard
workers
apartment
suburbs
village
town
shops
neighbors
community
neighborhood

Slide Down the Community Slide
Would you like to slide down the community sliding board? You can, but first you must climb to the top. How? By knowing your vocabulary words and what they mean. Each player turns the spinner and moves that number of spaces. If he can pronounce the word and tell what it means, he gets another turn. If not, he goes back to where he was. The first player to get to the top wins!

2. *Indian Chief.* Use laminated tagboard and draw an Indian head with a big feather headdress. Cut out separate feathers to be added to the headdress. (Directions are written beside the Indian head.) Answer cards and feathers may be stored in brown kraft envelopes and stapled to the back of the game.

INDIAN CHIEF

Put the feathers in the Indian's headdress by defining the words on the feathers.

Answer Card—Indian Chief

1. tribes—groups of Indians
2. canoe—a boat used by Indians
3. hominy—corn hulled and crushed, eaten boiled
4. moccasin—soft shoe of deerskin
5. trails—Indian paths through the forest
6. pirates—ship robbers
7. claim—announce that land is yours
8. governor—ruler of the colony
9. etc.

3. *Help Little Red.* Use colored tagboard; laminate. Cards and answer sheet may be stored in brown kraft enevelopes and stapled to back of game.

Help Little Red

Directions: 2 may play. You will need one person to check the answer sheet. Place cards face down. Little Red must go through the forest to get to the Chief's tepee. In order for him to get there you must help by drawing a card and answering questions, along the path. Make sure he doesn't run into a black bear.

Cards

1. What 3 groups of people live in North Carolina?

2. Who were the first people to live in North Carolina?

3. Indians lived in groups called _____.

4. Who was the first child born of English parents?

5. What were the names of the first 2 indians to visit England?

6. From what land did blacks come from?

7. What happened in 1776?

8. What was the first town in North Carolina?

9. Name some dances the colonists enjoyed.

10. What did the Stamp Act require?

Answers: Help Little Red

1. Indians, Europeans, Blacks
2. Indians
3. Tribes
4. Virginia Dare
5. Wanchese, Manteo
6. Africa
7. The United States became *free* from England.
8. Bath
9. Virginia Reel, Minuet
10. A stamp had to be bought to put on *all* papers.
   (Books, newspapers, documents, etc.)

4. *Community Helpers Task Cards*
A. *Matching Pictures with Words.* Match pictures of helpers with the words that identify each picture.   Colored shoestrings (or yarn) are used for matching and the back of each card is color-coded for self-correction.

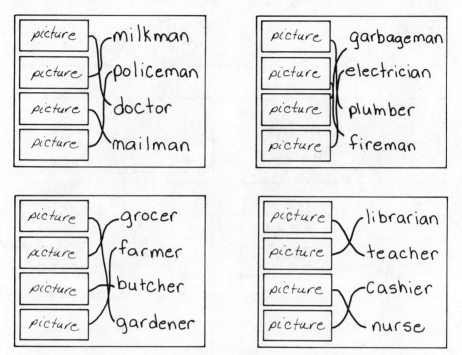

B. *Dot-to-Dot Helpers.* Outline any community helper, laminate it, and let the children draw in the picture with a grease pencil. This can then be erased for use by another child.

5. *Puzzle*: *"People and Their Jobs."* (Match the picture or name of a person with a picture or name of something he would use in his job.)

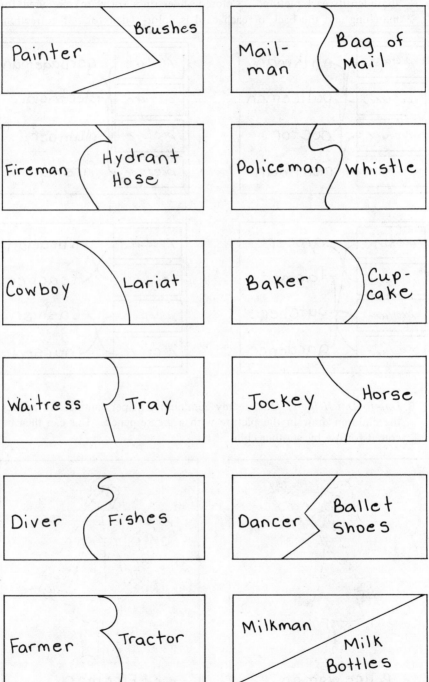

Some Objectives

To become a social being.

To accept and respect unique qualities of self and others.

To learn to make value judgments.

To explore various peoples around the world.

To develop an awareness of community.

To use resource materials to solve a challenge.

To see alternatives to situations as they arise.

To empathize with others who are different.

Suggested Activities

1. *Situation Cards.* When studying a particular area or topic, task cards can be developed which cause the child/children to be a part of that time or situation. An example for study of the west is listed below. This card is fairly simple; for older children, the card could delve into more complex social awareness.
   Situation:
   You are the parent of a family of five (3 girls, 2 boys). The other parent is visiting friends. It is the time of the early settlers in the west. It is nighttime. You hear the hoot of an owl. The cows are making noise out in the pasture. You know that the Indians have been attacking some settlers in the area.
   Questions:
   What is upsetting the cows? Was that really an owl hooting? What would you do? What could your community do to guard against Indians? Why did Indians attack settlers?
   These discussions are usually led by a parent or teacher. It is the responsibility of the group leader to ask questions that will make the children think more about the situation.
2. *Field Trips.* Through field trips children can experience social conditions beyond their ordinary realm. Trips could be taken to fire department, zoo, other schools, large industrial bakeries, construction sites, museums, etc. Videotaping the trip is an excellent way for the children to discuss what they saw on the trip. If your county or city system does not have videotaping equipment available, a movie of the trip could be made for the children to enjoy.
3. *Resource People.* For career awareness, invite persons of different occupations to visit the classroom and discuss their jobs. Parents should be utilized whenever possible.
4. *Communities.* Have the children build as many different communities as possible. Not only can children build minature communities, but they can build a community large enough to have dramatic/role play. (*Examples*: igloos, adobe huts, Indian teepee, straw huts, log cabins, etc.)

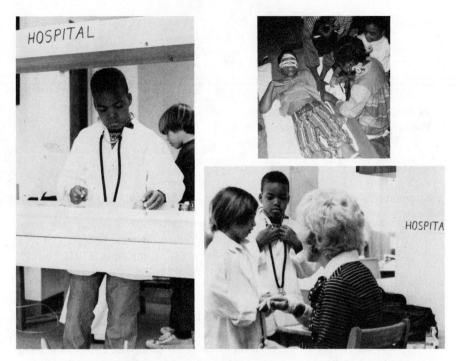

5. *Classroom Newspaper.* A class newspaper can be used for many purposes from current events to the classroom events. The editorial staff might be set up by examining several newspapers with the children and letting them decide what sections they would like to include in their paper. Some sections might be classroom, school, community, current national events, comics, sports, etc. The children might even decide on having a "Dear Abby." The paper could be published daily or weekly. (This can also be done on a short-term basis with all children having a chance to be editors.)

6. *Community Comparison.* Compare life in different communities. Have two groups and present them with the same situation to seek and answer for. Be sure to include situation group leaders. Some communities might be city/farm, present year/1900, ghetto/middle America, jungle village/home community, etc. Cards would describe life in the two communities.

7. *Role Playing.* Provide children with props such as fireman's gear, construction worker's helmet, soldier's uniform, turn-of-the-century clothes, etc. Ask them to guess who might wear the clothes and what they might do. The teacher must lead the children by asking questions to lead them in finding out about the personalities. After the children have found out about the people, let them role-play situations. The same idea could be carried out by showing the children tools of the trade such as plumber's friends, levels, stethoscope, toy cars, chalkboard, etc.

8. *Special Holidays.* How do different people in the same communities celebrate a holiday? From here, go to peoples around the world. "Is Halloween the same everywhere?" "Does everyone celebrate Christmas?" "Do they celebrate the 4th of July in England?" etc. Create role-playing situations. Make things in art such as piñatas and Halloween costumes. Cook holiday foods from around the world. Have a display, "Somebody has a holiday almost everyday." Discuss who is having a holiday and why.

9. *Films, Tapes.* Tapes could be used in place of a situation card. Tape-record stories about other people. Have films available in the classroom on topics that are currently being studied.

10. *Social Vocabulary.* Make language master cards for new words that are a part of the area being studied. Words could also be placed on a chart behind the language master. Illustrate cards when possible.

11. *Special Interest Areas.* Create usable displays to coordinate with current areas of study or as separate units. Some possible areas and ideas might be:

Drug Awareness:

Booklets: Blank booklets in the shape of a capsule, syringes, marijuana plant, letters LSD, etc. Children will use them to write or dictate about drugs.

Resource person. Person from narcotics squad to show various drugs and to alert children to the dangers of usage.

Language master. Use cards for developing vocabulary.

Filmstrip. Have available with related films.

Situation. As the unit draws to an end, bring a stranger on the school grounds who will attempt to sell drugs to children. The police might help with this.

Sex Education:

Use male and female small pets—rabbits, chickens, hamsters, guinea pigs, guppies, etc.

Chart: Watch the changes that occur during pregnancy. Things they might chart include weight (daily), amount of food eaten (daily), changes in habits, changes in appearance, etc.

12. *Family Size and History.*
   a. With a small group, chart each child's "home" family. Mothers might be designated with a blue stickman; fathers, orange; grandparents, green; brothers; red, sisters; yellow; others, purple. This helps children with the concept of family likenesses and differences and aids the teacher's understanding of each child.
   b. Provide family trees for children. Assist or let them fill in branches.

13. *Imaginary Trips.* Near the globe or a map, a task card might read, "Plan a trip to someplace. How would you travel to this place?" This is a good activity for cooperative effort from a multi-age group.

14. *Cook's Tour.* Through cooking experiences, children can travel to other lands. Parents of different nationalities might suggest and/or help with special "dishes."
15. *Mapping.* After a walk around the neighborhood or community, children can construct models of streets, landmarks, etc., on a card table, in the block area, or map on brown paper.
16. *Autobiographies.* Child tells teacher about himself. The teacher types and records the child's story.
17. *Elections.* Set up an election booth with a curtain. List main candidates (president, governor). Provide voting levers or ballots for voting. This is a good time to use politicians in the career awareness center.
18. *Public Safety.* Set up an imaginary street in the block center or on the wheel toy area of the playground. Allow children to drive without rules. Children offer solutions when problems arise.
19. *Division of Labor.*
    a. Use an ant farm or film loops on ants or bees. Children observe how ants and bees work as a society.
    b. Let a few students make baskets individually. Then assign each of these students a part of the basket-making task. Children discuss and compare what they like and dislike about the two ways of making baskets.
20. *Mini Field Trips.* A small group of children (1 or 2 from each teaching team) with a teacher or the principal visit a community resource person or place.

    Example: A greenhouse. Upon returning, children might write an experience story, report orally, plant seeds and chart growth, etc.
21. *Photos.* Use a Polaroid camera to take action shots of the children and to photograph people and places seen on field trips. These may be used to write or dictate experience stories, to fill current events section of paper, etc. Photos of child's family (past and present) give him some perspective on history.

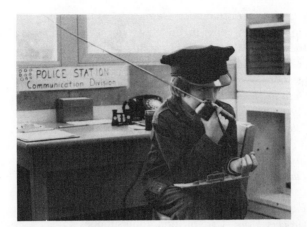

22. *Career Awareness Centers and Materials.* This may be separate or a part of another center. Books, tapes, films, or filmstrips on these careers can be used in all career awareness centers.

Examples:
   a. *Cosmetologist*—Wigs, rollers, clips and pins, comb, brush, mirror (turned horizontal) on table, hair dryer, apron, shampoo container
   b. *Barber*—Comb, scissors, shaving cream, apron, shampoo containers
   c. *Secretary*—Dictionary, telephone, typewriter, letters, paper, pen
   d. *Nurse*—First aid kit, thermometer, nurse's cap
   e. *Carpenter*—Tools, wood, bib overalls, yardstick, ruler, nails
   f. *Librarian*—Books, stamp, desk
   g. *Construction worker*—Wooden toys (bulldozer), hard hats, etc.
   h. *Truck driver*—Truck, traffic signs, cargo
   i. *Banker*—Puppet stage for window, checkbooks, play money, adding machine
   j. *Post office*—Window, stamps, letters, scales, pencil, money
   k. *Baker*—Stove, cooking utensils, apron, hat, etc.

23. *People and/or Community Resources.* Visit community site or have resource person come to the classroom. Make a special effort to visit factories, plants, etc., where parents work or invite them to come and share their skills or knowledge with the students.

Suggestions:

a. *Veterinarian*—Caring for sick pets

b. *Farm*—Animals, machines, gardens

c. *Lumber yard*—Tools, building equipment

d. *Stables*—Horses being shod

e. *Fish market*—Foods from water

f. *Farm stand*—Foods from land

g. *Pet shop*—Care of animals

h. *Florists*—Greenhouse, nursery–plant life

i. *Grocery store*—Care of food, food supplies

j. *Radio stations*—Transferring of ideas

k. *Zoos, museums*—animal life, historical events

24. *Museum, Hobby, or Special Interest Area.* Set up museum or hobby area in the classroom or hallways with beautiful exhibits.

25. *Population Education*: *Suggested Activities for Infusing Population Concepts into the Existing Primary Curriculum*

A. Language arts
- Flannel board stories illustrating various roles (family members, careers, etc.).
- Supplementing basal readers with discussions about alternative roles for adults (working women, one-parent families, single adults, etc.).
- Look through magazines to make books or collages about various population issues (crowding, alternative roles for women, pollution, etc.).
- Story starters in Creative Writing Centers about population issues.
- Field trips to feel the effects of crowding, listen for noise pollution, observe traffic, construction, trash (large shopping centers, busy airports and bus terminals, downtown district, industries). Use Language Experience charts to record results.
- Observe and list overcrowded conditions in the school (trailers, makeshift classrooms in the library, health room and hallways).
- Puppet shows to introduce various population concepts (advantages and disadvantages of small and large families, conservation, roles for women, etc.).
- Role playing and pantomime are fun ways to explore population issues while enhancing language development.

B. Mathematics
- Add, subtract, multiply sets of *people* rather than apples, trees, and lollipops.

- Chart the number of people in each child's family, discuss the average family size and compare and contrast various aspects of the largest family and the smallest family.
- Have children count and record the populations of their family, their neighbor's family, their class, their school, dogs and cats on their street, etc. Discuss *census*.
- Story problems such as "If a family of two drinks 2 gal. of milk a week, how much would a family of 4 drink?" (or 6, 8).
- Using one-to-one correspondence, divide 12 cookies between 2 children, 3 children, 4, 6.
- Introduce money concepts using problems that compare basic needs of small families with basic needs of large ones (lunch money, shoes, etc.).

C. Science
- Have animals in the classroom; observe and answer questions about reproduction frankly.
- Plant, grow, and take care of plants; chart growth, needs for sun, water, and air.
- Make bulletin boards illustrating land, air, and water pollution.
- Nature walks to observe effects of pollution in streams, dumping, etc.
- Make terrariums, aquariums to observe the balance of nature.
- Find ways to preserve the environment and practice them in the room (recycle paper and magazines, etc., to appropriate organizations, use both sides of writing paper, conserve electricity).
- One concrete experience the teacher must stage for the children in better understanding our dependence on electricity is disconnect all electrical equipment (A-V aids, lights, etc.) in the morning before the children arrive. Hold class under those conditions for a while; discuss and list all the uses of electricity in the room, look for alternatives.
- Have children inventory all electrical appliances in their homes.

D. Social studies
- Study families around the world, role-play different life-styles and roles.
- Use value-clarifying activities to enable children to act out and discuss their feelings and attitudes about controversial subjects.
- Explore the classroom for evidence of social and economic interdependence of countries (look at trademarks on items in the room; discuss vacations children have taken).
- Field trips to discover alternative roles for men and women: hospitals employ women doctors, researchers, and male nurses, clerks, etc. Resource people can be brought in to answer children's questions.

- Have various uniforms and wearing apparel in the housekeeping center for children to explore different roles themselves (military, doctor and nurse, wigs, etc.).
- Map skills can be used to discover population phenomenon. In the beginning of the year make a bulletin board display with a large U.S. map and place each child's picture with his name on the state he was born in; discuss *migration*. Starting with a state map showing topographical features, find suitable areas to live in, then plot the *density*. Children who are able and interested could do this with U.S. and world maps. Through an inquiry approach, children will discover that the inhabitable areas are becoming overpopulated.
- Give children the opportunity to work in various size groups and with all the other children, not just their "best friend."

Most important, each child should have many opportunities to realize his self-worth and the importance of his decisions on the quality of his life.

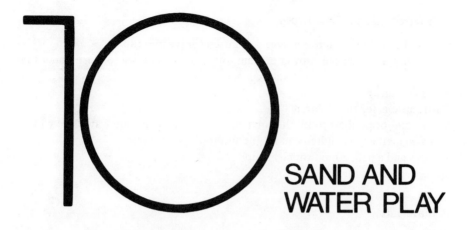

10 SAND AND WATER PLAY

There is something natural and basic about playing in sand and water—a tea party in the sun, a boat floating, or just pouring and sorting. The motivation is built in and the fun is there. Younger children might simply enjoy the sensorial experiences provided by sand and water; others may learn about letters by drawing in the sand, and still others can learn how cities are built by construction in the sand. As children work with sand and water, there are many possibilities for mathematics in measuring and filling, for language and communication in their dramatic play, and for science as they experiment with the qualities of their materials.

Environmental Resources

Sand and water table and/or a large galvanized (or plastic) tub
Sheets of plastic, an old shower curtain, or an absorbent rug to place under the
   tub
Scales (balance)
Plastic aprons for the children
A hose and/or pitchers to fill the tub (the teacher can mark the water line with a
   magic marker so children can fill the tub to the best level)
Sponges and a pail, a mop for clean-up
Storage space for materials

Materials

Permanent

   Plastic containers and lids (all sizes and shapes)
   Plastic dishes (cups, bowls, mugs, beakers)
   Measuring spoons and measuring containers (cup, 1/2 pint, pint, quart, gallon,
      liter)
   Weights (ounces, grams)
   Bubble pipes, eggbeaters and other mixers (whisks, spoons)
   Meat basters
   Corks, sponges
   Plastic eyedroppers
   Funnels of different sizes
   Sieves of all shapes and sizes, sprinkler tops on bottles
   Brushes of several sizes
   Flexible plastic tubing (of several diameters)
   Several lengths of pipe and hose
   Rolling pin, shells, stones
   Wheelbarrow, trowels, spoons, shovels, buckets, sticks, rakes, ladles, dump
      truck, sand combs

Expendable

   Straws
   Cakes of soap, Ivory Flakes, liquid soap
   Food coloring
   Tempera paint
   Small sponges
   Pieces of wood
   Styrofoam, cork
   Chart paper, markers
   Box of objects for sinking and floating (sponge, nail, rubber eraser, pencil,
      leaf, nickel, paper clip, rock, cork, crayon, twig, acorn, peanut, rubberband,
      wooden bead, lengths of sticks, spools, odd pieces of wood, scissors, etc.)

Teacher-made Materials

1. Tin cans with varying numbers of holes punched into the middle of the closed ends with a large nail. This can be used for both sand and water play.

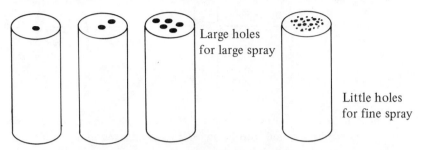

Large holes
for large spray

Little holes
for fine spray

2. Pie tins with holes punched into the bottom can be used for both sand and water play.

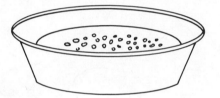

3. Cans with holes punched into the sides can be used for both sand and water play.

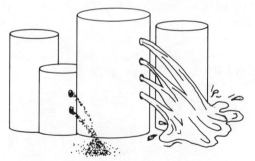

4. Large-sized detergent bottles (plastic) that are cut across the middle can be used for funnels in sand and water play.

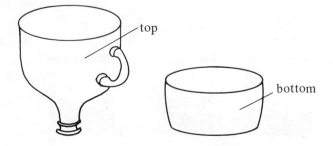

top

bottom

5. Balance for weighing sand and water.

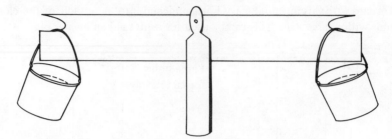

6. Cloth doll gives children experience in pouring. The doll is made of strong cloth, and sand is poured into her with a large tablespoon or wooden spoon. Drawstrings are at the top of her head for closing.

Sand Doll

7. Shakers made from Awake Orange Juice cans (because they have rubber tops) are filled to various levels with sand (both fine sand and gravel sand). These could also be used as shakers in music.

Sand Shakers

8. Shakers made from plastic medicine bottles. Round stick nailed to lid of jar for handle. Filled with sand. Can be used as a rhythm instrument.

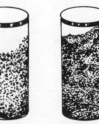

Sand Shakers

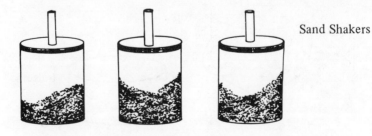

9. Materials for water and sand play.

Indoor play

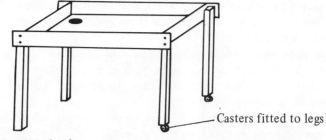

Casters fitted to legs

Large water trough of zinc or plastic with drain plug

Wood sand tray made of a 6″ × 1″ softwood frame and hardboard base strengthened with battens. Stood on chairs for play. Sand may be stored in tin cracker box.

Dishpan and towel on low table or box

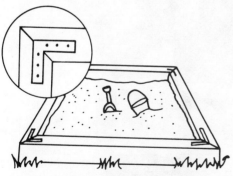

Another crude type of sand-box might be clinder blocks just put together to keep sand in an area. Children could sit on the blocks.

Wood-frame sandpit with metal strips across corners. Allow 6″ space for foot room from top to level of sand.

Tub of water on two crates

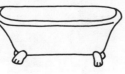

An old bathtub would be ideal for water play.

Some Objectives

To play creatively in the sand or water alone or with others.

To use the sand, water, and available materials to seek answers to open-ended questions.

To discover equivalences through the use of water and other materials.

To use large muscles while digging, hauling, and building with sand.

To classify materials that will and will not float; that are absorbent and nonabsorbent.

To further develop writing skills by labeling bottles, filled with sand or water and calling them (coke, milk, juice, etc.).

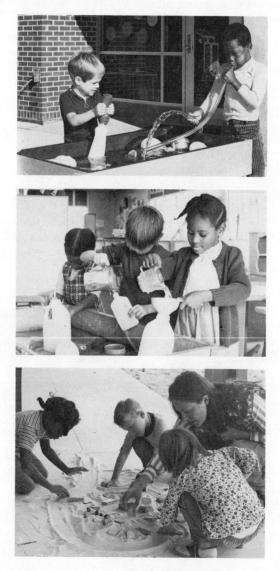

Suggested Activities

1. *Experiment with Food Color and Water.* Mix colors with water to discover how all colors are made from the primary colors (red, yellow, and blue).

Task Card

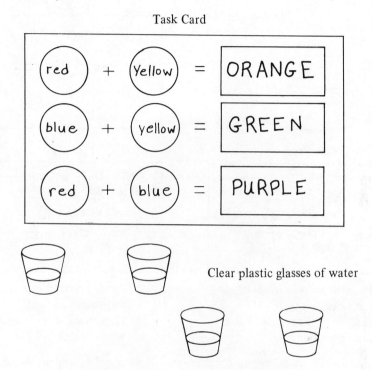

Clear plastic glasses of water

2. *Boat Races.* Divide pan into racing lanes. Children blow boats with straws. (Number boats for a math experience.) (Make chart.)

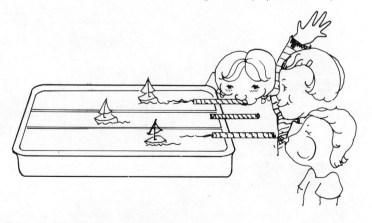

3. *Creative Water Painting.* Use brushes, sponges, or other materials to make wet imprints on the chalkboard.

4. *Task Cards.* Use teacher-made work cards or directions to suggest methods to help the child discover relationships between standard units of measurement and volumes of water, or sand and various sizes of containers.

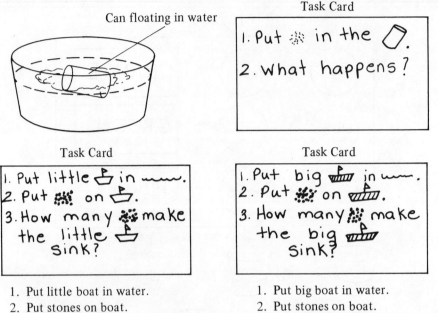

Can floating in water

Task Card

1. Put ✷ in the ⬭.
2. What happens?

Task Card

1. Put little ⛵ in ∼∼∼.
2. Put ✷ on ⛵.
3. How many ✷ make the little ⛵ sink?

Task Card

1. Put big ⛴ in ∼∼∼.
2. Put ✷ on ⛴.
3. How many ✷ make the big ⛴ sink?

1. Put little boat in water.
2. Put stones on boat.
3. How many stones make the little boat sink?

1. Put big boat in water.
2. Put stones on boat.
3. How many stones make the big boat sink?

5. *Floating and Sinking Experiment.* Have a collection of objects that sink and float. (See list under "Materials.") Two shoe boxes labeled "Things that sink" and "Things that float."

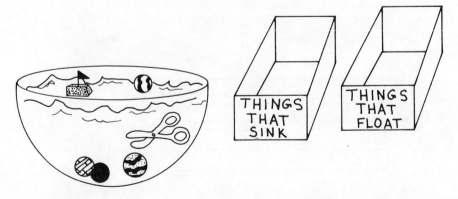

THINGS THAT SINK

THINGS THAT FLOAT

A large chart can also be made. Have the children paste (glue) all the "Things That Float" on one side and all the "Things That Sink" on the other.

6. *Therapeutic*. Use sand or water play as a therapeutic technique (playing for the sake of play and for relaxation and release of tensions).

7. *Water Play Related to Other Centers*. Other activities that involve water play are cleaning, washing dishes and/or clothes, imaginary cooking, etc.

8. *Vocabulary and Concept Development*. Encourage the child to describe what he is doing and to answer questions what, when, why, and how.

9. *Water Experiments*. Experiments dealing with:
   a. How water affects different properties (Kleenex, beans, sugar, clothes)
   b. The rate of water flow through various tubes and/or funnels and how and why different materials absorb water.

10. *Digging Activities*. Use the sand table or digging area outside with spoons, cups, trowels, sticks, and shovels to dig for enjoyment, to experiment with floating and damming, to build canals, etc.

11. *Map Study*. Use sand (in sand table) for simple map study. Streets, houses, stores, etc., can be constructed and placed on the sand or can be drawn using simply the child's finger.

12. *"Cooking."* Use sand and water for imaginary "cooking" experience. A recipe and directions might be placed over the tub to suggest this. The children may use this media for follow-up to role play in the home–living center.

13. *Letters in the Sand.* Use a tactile approach to learning letters, numbers, and shapes by having the children work in the sand or mix sand and water to form letters and numbers.

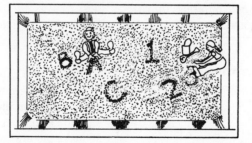

14. *Exploring*. Explore the various textures of dirt, temperature of water, and science of waves.

15. *Health*. In conjunction with the housekeeping, let the children give the dolls a bath or wash their clothes. This is a good way to teach about health practices.

16. *Outdoor Digging*. Have an unconstructed outdoor digging pile as a part of the topography of the outdoor area.

17. *Scales*. A pair of scales give extra opportunities for discovery; i.e., comparing the weight of wet and dry sand.

18. *Comparison of Size*. After considerable free play, a point to bring out is the size of two containers (*Example*: pint, quart). Which one holds the most? How many spoonfuls? Cups? Chart your results.

19. *Structure for Discovery*. Make sure there are containers that, although of different shapes, hold just about the same amount. The situation is then structured for discovery.
20. *Variety*. Children like variety in an activity. Food coloring, nontoxic detergent, or paints will stimulate new interest in water play.
21. *Transparent Materials*. As children experiment with volume and capacity, transparent containers allow the child to see more and to make better estimates.
22. *Talk*. Talk about how liquids and solids are measured in everyday situations (drink, medicine, flour, sugar) will offer beginning points for sand and water experimentation.
23. *Dictating or Writing Stories*. Write about experiences playing in the sand. (i.e., "How I Made Muffins." "The Sand Village," "If I Were a Sand Castle I Would . . . ")
24. *Aquarium*. Make an aquarium with sand on the bottom. Plant water plants in the sand. Use siphon tube so plants and sand do not get disturbed.
25. *Sandpaper*. Children can sand wood ships or toys (boats, airplanes, trucks) from the woodworking center.
26. *Measuring Water for Eating and Drinking*. Make Jello, Kool–aid, popsickles, and ice cubes.
27. *Rain Observation*. Collect rain in a pan. Then pour it into a glass quart jar. On another day do the same thing. Compare which day it rained the most.
28. *Planting and Watering Activities*.

Planting and Watering Task Cards (Done over a period of a few days.)

1. Put soil in a cup.
2. Plant a seed in the soil.
3. Put water on the seed.
4. Look at the cup every day.
5. Make pictures of what you see.

 No water

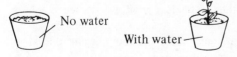 With water

Watering Plants Task Card

1. Plant 2 seeds in 2 paper cups.
2. Put water in 1 cup.
3. Do not put water in the other cup.
4. Which seeds grow?

1. Water 1 plant.
2. Do not water the other (2).
3. What happened?
4. Then water both plants.
5. What happens?

29. *Water Glass Chimes.* Fill glasses of the same size with different amounts of water. Strike rims of glasses lightly with various instruments.

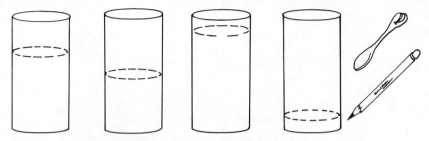

30. *Observation of Colored Water.* Color a glass of water. Place a stalk of celery in it. Have children observe how the colored water rises up through the celery.

31. *Plastic Puppets.* Children can use these puppets in water play (ducks, dolphin, fish, etc.).
32. *Listening Experience.* Boil water in a kettle. This can be a listening experience as they listen to the boiling water and the whistle.
33. *Melt Snow and Ice.*
34. *Teach Unit on Weather.*
35. *Ripples.* Throw stones and rocks in water at local lake to see the ripple effect. Perhaps some can make a stone skim the water.
36. *Discuss* the role of the plumber as a community leader.
37. *Take a Visit* to the basement of the school to see the water pipes.
38. *Cut Out Pictures* of water in its various forms from magazines.
39. *Water Play—Art Related Activities*
    A. Making boats for water play
       1. Spool boat

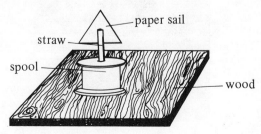

2. Scrap lumber boats
3. Newspaper boats
4. Leaf boats
5. Jar lid boats

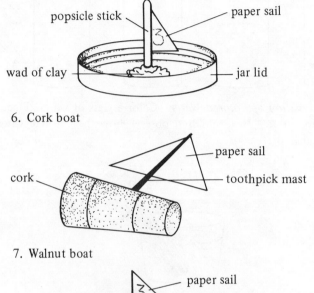

6. Cork boat

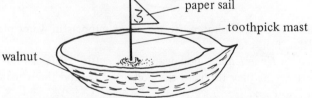

7. Walnut boat

B. Beanbags filled with sand.
C. Write name and draw pictures in the sand.

D. Paint pictures with water on the sidewalk or chalkboard with a clean paint brush.

E. Sand Painting. Add 1/4 paint powder to 1 part sand and combine in large shakers. Children shake on paper they have covered with paste.

F. Elmer's Glue sand painting. Design a picture on a colored piece of construction paper with Elmer's Glue. Scatter sand on top, then brush off. Sand remains where glue was.

G. Sandpaper numeral charts

H. Sandpaper pictures

Colored crayon or chalk may be rubbed over sandpaper color.

I. Painting with water colors. Children learn that depending on how much water they use, their color will get darker or lighter.

J. Sand candles. Make a roundish indention in the sand. Fill with melted (colored) wax. Put in wick. Wait till dry. Remove from sand. Brush off. Rather expensive when sold in candle shops.

11 WOODWORKING

Woodworking or carpentry is basically engaging in purposeful play and/or work activity that encourages using the hands, solving problems, and developing mathematical concepts. The creative potential of this center is unlimited. Constructing materials of cardboard and wood provides opportunities to create abstract and fanciful structures. Classroom unity and pride are quite naturally developed as children work together to build a completed product.

Environmental Resources

Workbench or table with—
　Height proportionate to size of children
　Top that allows for painting and/or hammering without fear of damage
　Space sufficient to allow movement
　Rollers to allow it to be moved from the inside to outside
Storage space—a tool cabinet with pegs, shelves, drawers, and containers for other
　materials

Equipment

Hammer—7 oz. claw
Screwdrivers—4″
"C" clamps—4″
Nails—variety of penny and heads
Vise for workbench
Screws—assorted size and types
Hooks
Ruler, measuring tape, and yardstick
Planes—block and smoothing
Saws—hand crosscut, coping (for curves and designs), keyhole
Pliers—combination, 6″
Sawhorse
File—cabinet, 1/2 round 8″
File card for cleaning file
Brace and bit
Hinges
Monkey wrench
Hand drill and bits
Wire cutter
Rasp and file
T—square
Miter box
Paint scraper

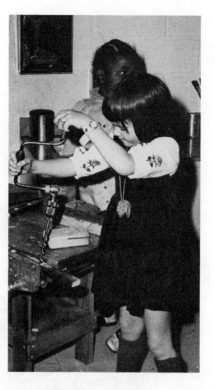

Materials

Wood scraps—many varied shapes and sizes
    Soft white pine or spruce
    Some finished and unfinished wood
    Molding and doweling
    Plywood
Cardboard
    Tri-wall
    Large posterboard boxes

Supplies

Pencils, scissors, string, wallpaper scraps, tacks, tape, leather, wire, chicken wire,
    paper clips, glue
Small wheels, tongue depressors, bottle caps
Formica, tile, linoleum
Sandpaper, paint, shellac, brushes
Hinges, knobs, nails, screws, nuts, bolts
Pulleys, rope
Broom, dustpan, rags

Some Objectives

To create using wood as a media of expression.

To discover relationships of quantity, equality, inequality, and proportionate comparisons while building and constructing with wood and other materials.

To communicate, plan, and work cooperatively with others to solve common problems.

To use building to release emotions and/or as a means of nonverbal expression.

To develop fine muscles by working with hammer and nails and large muscles by working with saw, lifting, etc.

To improve eye-hand coordination by manipulating tools.

Suggested Activities

1. *Resource Person.*   Invite a local carpenter (preferably a parent or relative of one of your students) to demonstrate proper usage of major tools, importance of measuring for proper proportions, how to smooth wood with sandpaper, etc.
2. *Field Trips.* Plan field trips to a construction site and/or a lumber yard.
3. *Large Tree Stump.* Add a large tree stump inside or outside to this center to use for hammering.
4. *Task Cards.* Use cards with suggestions of things the children can make.
5. *Ideas for Using Wood.* Simple objects such as animals, boats, etc., can be made by children. Children can build their own creative structures; older children may use simple pictorial directions. The finished product may be painted.

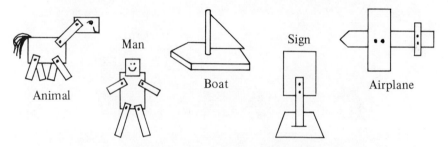

6. *Ideas for Using Cardboard.* Cardboard can be especially purchased for this or can be obtained as industrial scrap.
    Stool—Make base from large tube, top from thin plywood or tri-wall. Fasten with tape or glue, or use small telephone spools.
    Table—Same as above using several tubes for the base.
    Storage containers—Fasten several tubes together.
7. *Mobiles.* These may be made by using several scraps of decorated wood and cardboard.

12
EVALUATING
AND RECORDING
OPEN LEARNING

Evaluation in an open or informal learning environment is based on the individual child's own work. There is a trend away from grades or marks, test scores, and testing periods and an emphasis on what the child is doing and how he does it. The open learning environment is one where discovering and expanding individual capabilities is valued and where school experiences are different for individual children. Evaluation then is individual and children help to plan and evaluate some of their own learning.

● Record keeping in an open environment is very important; accurate and detailed reports of the individual child's developmental levels and what he is doing must be kept. These records may take many forms, among them anecdotal notes, files of children's work, records of formal and informal tests, checklists, and, most important, teacher observation—both informal and systematic and often over a long period of time.

● Evaluation is for the child as well as for the teacher. Not only does evaluation tell the teacher if the child is ready to move on to another concept or if there are learning gaps that need special attention, but it allows for the child to make mistakes and errors. Correct answers are viewed as only one aspect of learning, as errors are desirable when they offer information necessary for further learning. Teachers should encourage excellence of individual students. ● Teachers may request that work be improved; however, this is not seen as failure. ● Rather, the request is viewed as constructive criticism with the teacher emphasizing good aspects of the work, those that are not so good, and those that could be improved.

Two considerations are necessary in evaluating pupil progress in an open learning environment: the ways and instruments necessary for assessing student progress and the ways and instruments for reporting this progress.

Since evaluation in an open learning environment is an ongoing process, the teacher, in addition to being a guide and resource person, must also be a very keen observer. The choices made by the child give the teacher insight into the child's learning. What he rejects or ignores offers clues to whether the child and the teachers are succeeding in what they are trying to do. Did the child seem interested in exploring the new materials in the math center? How long did he remain in the center attempting to solve the problems? What activity did he choose when he finished reading with the teacher? Did the child seem interested enough to want to share it with a classmate or an observer in the room? ● Through observation of activities, discussions with students, and listening to students talk to each other, the teacher has a basis for formulating future work. In addition, students share in the responsibility of deciding some of the things they are interested in learning.

Because there are so many things going on simultaneously in an open classroom, the teacher must keep a record of activity if there is to be a continuum of purposeful learning. This record may contain the amounts of time spent at particular tasks, the different activities in which children participate, the quality of the participation (i.e., learning task cards completed, gaps in learning that imply individual or small group work with the teacher, the variety of activities including cognitive, social, emotional, and physical growth), and recommended next steps. This record might be obtained through direct observation of individual students and through written work that would also indicate individual achievement.

● Student records may be kept in folders or notebooks and on index cards. The information should be concise and descriptive; it should be dated and compared monthly with changes in individual achievement indicated. Opposite is an example of how an individual record showing the progress of a six-year-old might appear.

Records should indicate general behavior patterns as well as academic achievement. Pleasant or disturbing family occurrences, illnesses, accidents and highlights at school should all be noted as these may be important in assessing the child's overall development. These records indicate the social interaction and emotional development to which academic learning is greatly related.

Class records, family grouping records, or team records must also be kept. Through these records an analysis may be made of the activities shared by a larger number of children. The students may help to keep these records, often in the form of charts or lists indicating centers visited; stories read, told or written; special projects undertaken; commercial and teacher-made games played; and learning task cards completed. Observation of this record should reveal balance in a variety of areas; if lack of variety is indicated steps can be taken to prevent this from happening.

Michael B.

9/21 Art and Experience Story—Drew a picture of a picnic (complete with football playing and eating toasted marshmallows) which took place during the summer vacation, dictated a story, consisting of five sentences, to a parent aide about this experience. Story and pictures reflect creativity as well as good sentence structure.

9/22 Science—Is very much interested in reading and looking at pictures about animals. Together we made up a contract of work for him to complete on beavers and alligators. (Contract to be filed in his folder.)

9/25 Math—Has worked for several days with Cuisenaire rods and learning task cards numbered 15-24. Self-correcting cards indicate good progress. Must give him individual achievement test in a few days.

9/30 Blocks—Michael has been the leader in designing the city of Washington, D.C., in the block building center. This interest stems from a recent family trip there. Additional unit blocks were borrowed from Mrs. Smith's room next door in order to complete the Washington Monument structure. Labels have been placed on all the structures. Filmstrip, books and records, and language master task cards on Washington have been added to the listening and viewing center. Michael seems more interested in staying in the block center and constructing rather than reading and viewing. Must be encouraged to visit the listening and viewing center.

10/4 Writing—Had to be encouraged to do his own writing about a recent field trip to the children's museum. Has no trouble remembering his experiences, or even adding interesting information to them; needs help in making his writing neater.

10/8 Reading—Is reading very well independently in the book *Adventures At Sea*, 3. Encouraged him to take this book home to read to his parents. Must work with him on his interfering with Tommy and Susan during math skill group.

10/13 Social Behavior—Michael is very popular among his classmates in spite of his inability at this time to control his temper if things don't always go his way. We're working on this, paying special attention to rewarding, through praise, his positive actions. Has shown some improvement and is aware that his teachers and parents are concerned about helping him with this.

Students should also be encouraged to keep records through their own diaries and activities. This diary will help the child understand his own progress; it will help the teacher learn what seems to interest the child most or gives him the greatest satisfaction. Accuracy is not as important in keeping a diary as is the recording of how a child feels about the work he is doing as well as about himself.

Records or logs may also be used by the child to help him plan activities he intends to undertake during the day. Throughout or at the end of the day, he may summarize his accomplishments. He may also wish to have conferences with the teacher or team of teachers regularly anytime during the day. Following are examples of records or logs that may be used for recording activities or centers visited. It should be noted that there are a variety of ways to help children record their daily activities. Some records are quantitative only in nature and serve only to summarize the amount of activity. Others include qualitative judgments on the part of the student and/or teacher.

Through the use of records such as the ones presented here, the teachers' additional records, and the children's diaries and logs, teachers should be able to identify each child's general achievements in skills and the areas that indicate special help is needed. Also, teachers should be able to know the kinds of work each child has been doing and how he has progressed in these areas. In addition to the teachers and the children, however, a third party must also be involved—the parents.

Parents play a vital role in the evaluation of each child, from the beginning of the school year and throughout a child's educational program. Home information (i.e., early experiences and language development, position in the family, interests that the child has at home, behavior and attitude among family members, etc.) is necessary in helping teachers understand the child, as these experiences often affect the child's school experience. Parent-teacher conferences should become a regular part of the school program as they are helpful not only in keeping parents informed of their child's growth but also in engaging their support in school activities. Parents are entitled to know exactly what the child is learning and what he might be having difficulty doing. Samples of the child's work should be shown and analyzed during the conference periods. Along with the records the teachers have kept (both individual and total group) and the records and diaries that the individual children have kept, the parent-teacher conferences should provide occasions for shared evaluation.

Obviously, evaluation of individual learning is the most important aspect of a school assignment program. It is also important, however, for the teacher to regularly assess the learning environment where children are living and growing during the many hours spent at school. Following is a checklist that is designed to help teachers evaluate the effectiveness of a learning environment for young children.

Sample 1

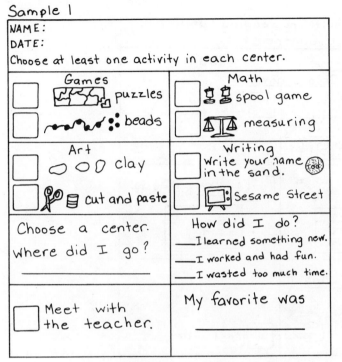

NAME:
DATE:
Choose at least one activity in each center.

Games	Math
☐ puzzles	☐ spool game
☐ beads	☐ measuring

Art	Writing
☐ clay	☐ Write your name in the sand.
☐ cut and paste	☐ Sesame Street

Choose a center. Where did I go? _____	How did I do? ___ I learned something new. ___ I worked and had fun. ___ I wasted too much time.
☐ Meet with the teacher.	My favorite was _____

Sample 2

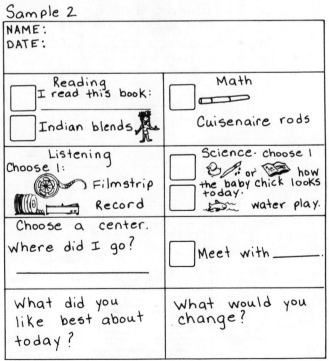

NAME:
DATE:

Reading ☐ I read this book: ☐ Indian blends	Math ☐ Cuisenaire rods
Listening Choose 1: ☐ Filmstrip ☐ Record	Science- choose 1 ☐ or how the baby chick looks today. ☐ water play.
Choose a center. Where did I go? _____	☐ Meet with _____.
What did you like best about today?	What would you change?

Sample 3

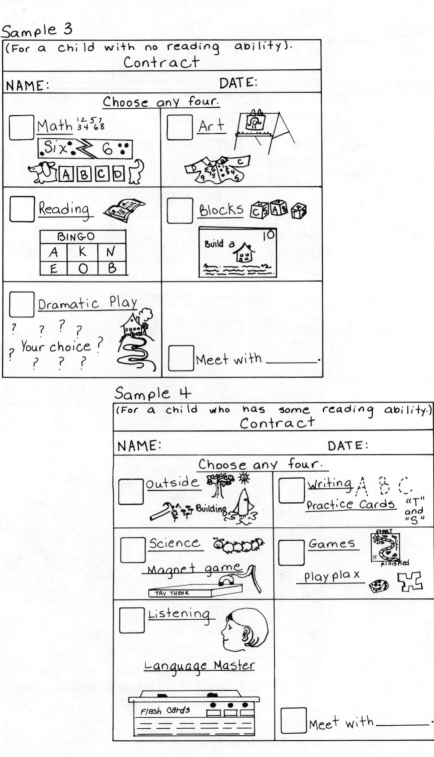

(For a child with no reading ability).

Contract

NAME: DATE:

Choose any four.

☐ Math   ☐ Art

☐ Reading   ☐ Blocks

Build a ... 10

☐ Dramatic Play

? ? ? ? Your choice ? ? ? ?

☐ Meet with _____.

Sample 4

(For a child who has some reading ability.)

Contract

NAME: DATE:

Choose any four.

☐ Outside   Building   ☐ Writing A B C Practice Cards "T" and "S"

☐ Science   Magnet game   TRY THESE   ☐ Games   Play plax

☐ Listening   Language Master   Flash cards

☐ Meet with _____.

Sample 5

Name:	Week of:

☐ Reading _Monday_	☐ Reading _Tuesday_
☐ Writing	☐ Writing
☐ Math	☐ Math
☐	☐
☐	☐
☐ with the teacher.	☐ with the teacher.

☐ Reading _Wednesday_	☐ Reading _Thursday_
☐ Writing	☐ Writing
☐ Math	☐ Math
☐	☐
☐	☐
☐ with the teacher.	☐ with the teacher.

☐ Reading _Friday_	How Did I Do?
☐ Writing	☐ I went to lots of centers.
☐ Math	☐ I learned something new.
☐	☐ I need to work harder.
☐	☐ I liked _____ best.
☐ with the teacher.	

Sample 6

Contract

Name:	Date:

Choose any 3 of the 4 centers.

☐ <u>Art</u>   Make one of these:
A burlap flower, stitchery,
A design, weaving.

☐ <u>Math</u>   Play one of the games

☐ <u>Reading</u>   Read a book about an animal.

☐ <u>Writing</u>   Do one of these:
(1) Make up a story using a story starting card (5 sentences.)
(2) Practice your writing using task card: numbers 5-8

☐ Meet with _____.

What did you like best about today?
What would you change?

Sample 7

Contract	
Name:	Date:

Choose any four.

☐ **Math**

Play the marching addition game. Keep your own score.

☐ **Art**   Choose one:
(1) Junk collage.
(2) Pipe cleaner flowers.
(3) Paint a picture.
(4) Stitch a picture.

☐ **Science**
- Look at the book "Insects in our world".
- Find the centipede.
- Make a list of things you learned about centipedes.
- Make an egg carton centipede.

☐ **Outside**
   Choose one.
(1) Build something that moves.
(2) Write or draw something on the sidewalk that shows how you feel.
   (Use color chalk)

☐ **Writing**
- Choose a picture.
- Write a story. You may use chart paper.
- Read it to a friend.
- Put it in the center.

☐ Meet with _____.

Sample 8

Name:		Date:

Centers

Art ☐   Lang. Arts ☐   Science ☐
Writing ABC ☐   Home ☐   Listening ☐
Math 1+1=2 ☐   Reading ☐   Sand ☐

Tools ☐   Cozy corner ☐

Write about what you did in centers today.

Sample 9

CENTERS

Reading corner
1. Telephone Activity
2. Magazine Activity
3. Weekly Activity
4. Read and do follow-up
   Follow-up: _____

Math Center
1. Geo. boards
2. Cuisenaire Rods Activity
3. Tic = Tac = Toe
4. Weight Activity
5. Measure Activity
6. Add with books

Creative Writing
1. News in Suite 9
2. What am I dreaming?
3. Write a book!
4. My pet.
5. Write a cartoon.
6. Write about a picture.

Spelling Center
1. Play spill + spell
2. Crossword puzzle
3. Play spelling fun
4. Secret code
5. Tic = TAC = Toe
6. "ow" card

Language Center
1. ABC order folder
2. My weekend
3. Find action words
4. Find football words
5. Find homonyms
6. Your choice...
   I choose _____

Science Center
1. Read a "Fishy" book.
2. Crossword puzzles
3. Adult animal activity
4. Insect flashcards
5. Choose an insect
   Write 5 facts about
   it. Draw it's picture.

Sample 10

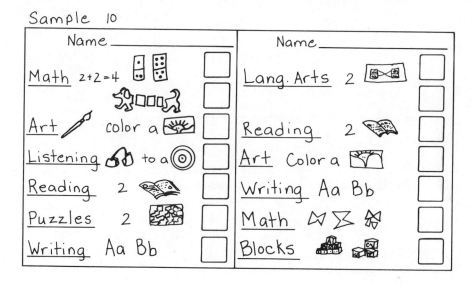

Name _____

Math 2+2=4

Art — color a

Listening — to a

Reading 2

Puzzles 2

Writing Aa Bb

Name _____

Lang. Arts 2

Reading 2

Art Color a

Writing Aa Bb

Math

Blocks

Sample 11

Name: _____

	MON.	TUES.	WED.	THURS.	FRI.
Title of Book and Story					
Pages Read					
Follow-up Activity					
Oral Activity					

Sample 12

Name: _____

CENTERS

MON.	TUES.	WED.	THURS.	FRI.

Writing -Aa---
Reading
Math 2+2=4
Language Arts
Puzzles
Science
Home
Art
Listening
Research
T.V.
Puppets
Blocks

Sample 13

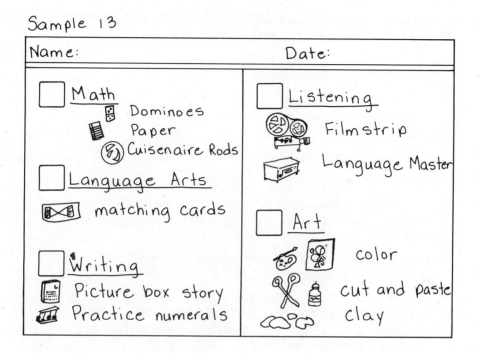

Name:	Date:
☐ <u>Math</u> 　　🁢 Dominoes 　　▦ Paper 　　🜋 Cuisenaire Rods ☐ <u>Language Arts</u> 　▧ matching cards ☐ <u>Writing</u> 　📖 Picture box story 　🎞 Practice numerals	☐ <u>Listening</u> 　🎥 Filmstrip 　▭ Language Master ☐ <u>Art</u> 　🎨🖼 color 　✂🧴 cut and paste 　☁ clay

Sample 14

Name		MON.	TUES.	WED.	THURS.	FRI.
	Skill Group					
	Language Skill					
	Scholastic					
	Handwriting					
C E N T E R S	Science 🦋					
	Creative Writing					
	Spelling　ABC					
	Language Games					
	Math　2+2=4					
	Listening 🎧					
	Reading Enjoyment 🚗					
	Exploration					
	Media Center					
	Social Studies					

A CHECKLIST FOR EVALUATING A GOOD LEARNING ENVIRONMENT FOR YOUNG CHILDREN

Teacher–Child Relationships

Yes No

1. Do you serve as a guide, facilitator of learning, resource person rather than a dispenser of information? — —

2. Do you have respect for and trust children? — —

3. Do you offer suggestions in a positive, sincere manner? — —

4. Do you circulate among the children—encouraging them, asking them individual questions, and giving each child individual attention every day? — —

5. Do the children understand their responsibilities and are they encouraged to be independent? — —

6. Do you believe that children respond to genuine experience of trust with positive, productive, and enjoyable behavior, and that they respond to lack of trust and confidence with destructive, hostile, and immature behavior? — —

7. Do you make sure that each child succeeds in something every day? — —

8. Do you operate in a manner that suggests that joy in learning, respect for others, and learning how to learn are more important than acquisition of specific subject information? — —

9. Are the children secure in what they know and not frightened by what they do not know? — —

10. Do you really *listen* to questions raised by children and do you *answer* them or seek to help individual children find the answer on the appropriate level? — —

Program

1. Is the program organized to allow for individual differences in pace, style, and range of learning? — —

2. Are many opportunities provided for learning through the senses—feeling, hearing, tasting, smelling, seeing? — —

3. Are children free to select many of their own learning activities by using learning centers that are available to them? — —

4. Are the children encouraged to talk to each other, ask questions, and seek their own answers? — —

Yes   No

5. Are there a variety of exciting firsthand experiences available for the children where they can make choices and produce on their own?   ___ ___

6. Is an "integrated day" in operation, on which there are no class lessons based on prescribed time allotments, but rather a great variety of experiences are available in the creative, intellectual, artistic, and physical areas?   ___ ___

7. Are children learning from each other—by observing, imitating, and teaching one another?   ___ ___

8. Are the children planning and evaluating their activities?   ___ ___

9. Are children given freedom to learn by exploring, discovery, inquiry, and experimenting rather than by being given facts or direct answers to their questions?   ___ ___

10. Are individual and small-group activities encouraged rather than total group instruction?   ___ ___

Materials and Equipment

1. Is there a wide variety of materials, supplies, and equipment for children to work with which accommodates different ages, abilities, and interests?   ___ ___

2. Are children encouraged to interact with or act upon their environment using many open-ended and self-corrective materials?   ___ ___

3. Are children encouraged to supply some of their own materials so that their interests are appreciated and fully incorporated into the program?   ___ ___

4. Are materials available which ensure development of both fine and gross motor skills?   ___ ___

5. Are materials organized and do they have a definite place so that children know right where to find them and also can put them away immediately after use in the appropriate place?   ___ ___

6. Are the children free to use the equipment by themselves and do they know how to properly care for it?   ___ ___

7. Are informal, teacher-made and child-made materials encouraged and utilized as well as commercially made materials?   ___ ___

8. Are materials and equipment safe and durable and are they used outdoors throughout the day just as appropriately as indoors?   ___ ___

Yes   No

9. Are there many materials that are concrete and sensory and can be counted, arranged, and rearranged; are these things that can be taken apart and put together again?   —   —

Physical Environment

1. Are the classrooms decentralized or divided into a variety of learning centers, rather than in straight rows of desks or tables and chairs?   —   —

2. Is the furniture arranged so that a number of large work surfaces are available?   —   —

3. Is the classroom a beautiful place with a warm, inviting, home-like atmosphere?   —   —

4. Are there a variety of learning centers, in areas such as language arts, math and science, art and music, housekeeping, woodworking, sand and water, listening and viewing, a creative corner, and a quiet area with a piece of colorful carpet and/or some pillows?   —   —

5. Is there adequate space for active children to explore, create, and move around freely?   —   —

6. Are there storage areas with an adequate place for each child to put his wraps, completed work and projects, and other possessions?   —   —

7. Are the toilet and water facilities adequate and convenient for children?   —   —

8. Are the rooms well heated, lighted, and ventilated?   —   —

9. Is there provision for an easy flow of activities between outdoors and indoors and is the out-of-doors used throughout the day as a part of the total living–learning environment?   —   —

10. Is the outdoor area adequate for free play, organized games, and quiet play?   —   —

Outdoor Learning Environment

1. Is the outdoors utilized as part of the total living–learning environment in conjunction with the indoors as an extension of the classroom?   —   —

2. Are the children free to move outside as a part of an integrated day, and are the experiences enriching rather than restricting?   —   —

3. Is there an entrance into the school from the outside so that

Yes No

games, materials, and equipment can be moved in and out easily? — —

4. Are open-ended materials available for children to use in their own creative ways, i.e., boxes, barrels, rubber tubes, wood strips, kegs with rubber tops for drums. — —

5. Is there a hard surface area that would be appropriate for block play, play with wheel toys, bouncing ball, and other activities? — —

6. Is there a balance of sunny and shaded areas so that the children might choose either? — —

7. Is there a grassy area that would provide a soft area for sitting together for a story, playing, or running? — —

8. Is the outdoor environment safe—free from glass and sharp metal? — —

9. Is there a mixture of homemade, inexpensive equipment (ropes, tires, telephone spools, sewer pipes, beanbags, newspaper ball, etc.) and commercial equipment (jungle gyms, wheeled toys, slides, and other stationary play equipment, climbing and reaching apparatus, rockers, etc.)? — —

10. Is there a sandbox with buckets, shovels, various containers, water, blocks, measuring containers of various sizes and shapes, toys so that math concepts and imaginative and dramatic play will be fostered? — —

11. Is there an adequate woodworking table with appropriate tools (hammer, saws, nails, screwdrivers, plane, chisel, jigsaw, vise, drill, clamp, file, sandpaper, measuring sticks), a variety of sizes and shapes of wood pieces, and a sawhorse available for use by the children? — —

12. Is there an area provided for water play with a variety of materials (boats, sponges, corks, funnels, rubber hoses, plastic containers for measuring, eggbeaters, liquid detergent, objects that sink and float) available so that the children can explore, analyze, and discover some simple math and science concepts? — —

13. Are easels available for outdoor painting and is there a roller table (or cart) for paints, brushes, and other art supplies that can be readily wheeled to the outdoor area for art? — —

14. Is there an adequate area for block building outside (preferably a cement area) and is there a roller cart or bin for rolling blocks from the block center to the outside area? — —

15. Is there evidence of growing things (vegetable gardens, flower

Yes No

gardens, potted plants) that have been planted and cared for by the children? —   —

16. Are there outdoor animals in cages or pens which are kept as pets or kept for observation? —   —

17. Do the equipment and materials provided encourage children to do something based on their own ideas rather than just watch it operate? —   —

18. Are the equipment and space adequate for the development of motor skills and muscular coordination? —   —

19. Is the outdoor area accessible so as to facilitate supervision and minimize the possibility of accidents (preferably large windows from floor to ceiling)? —   —

20. Are adequate equipment and space provided for dramatic play (tree house, fort, Indian teepee, raised platforms, stripped–down car, rows of wooden crates, logs, trees, stumps, outdoor theater, little houses, or "in and out" places where the children can crawl through, climb in and out of)? —   —

21. Is there an outside storage area and is the equipment organized and stored so that children know where it is and where to put it away? —   —

22. Is there an outside covered area or roof so that activity can go on even on drizzly days? —   —

23. Are the children given the opportunity to work and play outside alone and in small groups and both quietly and actively? —   —

24. Is there a nature environment with trees, plants, and flowers so the children can explore, discover, analyze, and learn about the science of plants and animals? —   —

25. Is there climbing equipment and apparatus to help develop large body muscles in the arms and legs? —   —

26. Are there balancing beams, logs, posts, or tree stumps so that the children can develop a sense of bodily balance? —   —

27. Is there sufficient and, if possible, sliding apparatus to help develop a sense of motor direction? —   —

28. Are there interesting and challenging swings that can help develop arm and leg muscles, such as "knotted rope swing" or a tire-swing? —   —

29. Is there a slide or smooth pole that the children can climb up and slide down? —   —

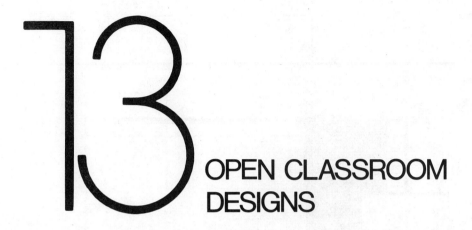

13 OPEN CLASSROOM DESIGNS

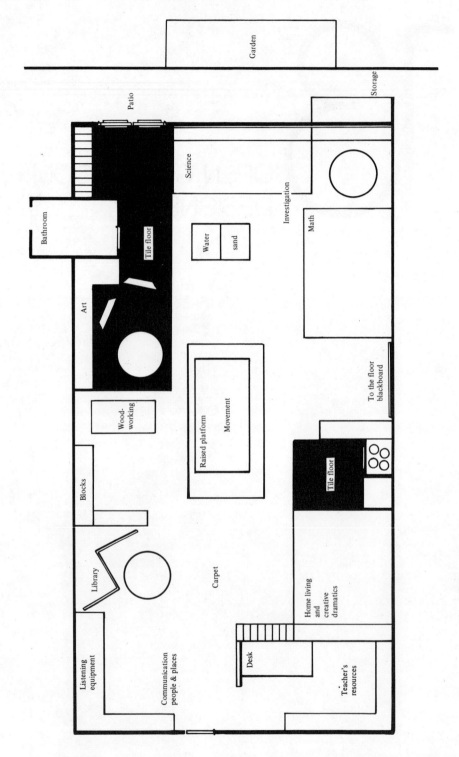

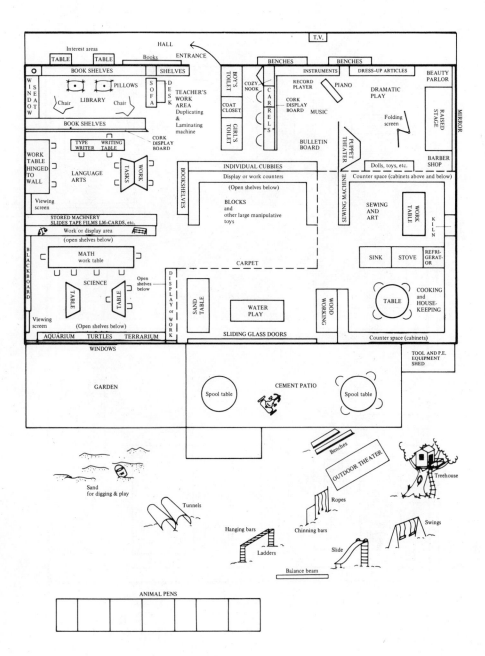

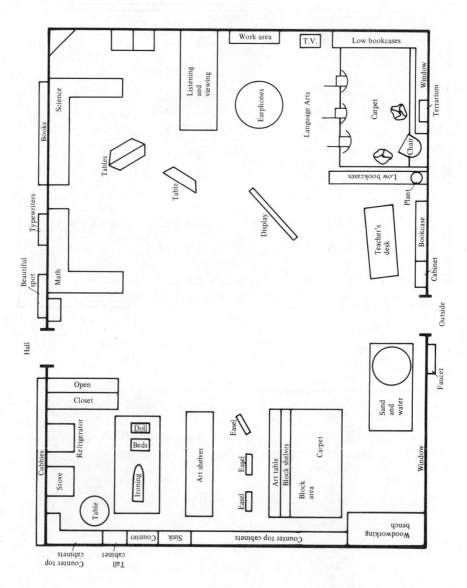

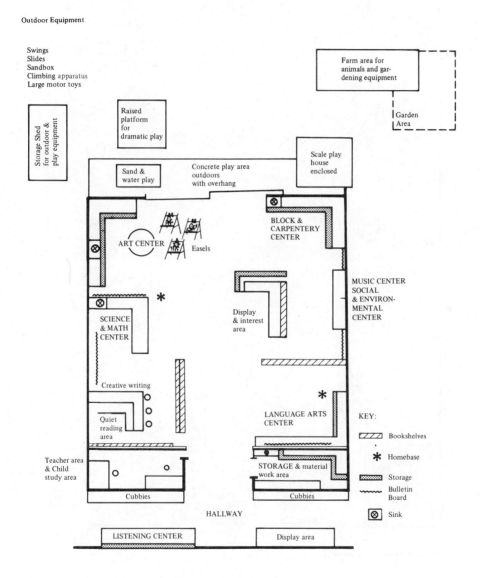

Outdoor Equipment

Swings
Slides
Sandbox
Climbing apparatus
Large motor toys

Storage Shed for outdoor & play equipment

Raised platform for dramatic play

Sand & water play

Concrete play area outdoors with overhang

Scale play house enclosed

Farm area for animals and gardening equipment

Garden Area

ART CENTER   Easels

BLOCK & CARPENTERY CENTER

MUSIC CENTER SOCIAL & ENVIRON- MENTAL CENTER

Display & interest area

SCIENCE & MATH CENTER

*

Creative writing

Quiet reading area

LANGUAGE ARTS CENTER

*

Teacher area & Child study area

STORAGE & material work area

Cubbies

Cubbies

KEY:

▨▨ Bookshelves

* Homebase

▨▨ Storage

〰〰 Bulletin Board

⊗ Sink

HALLWAY

LISTENING CENTER

Display area

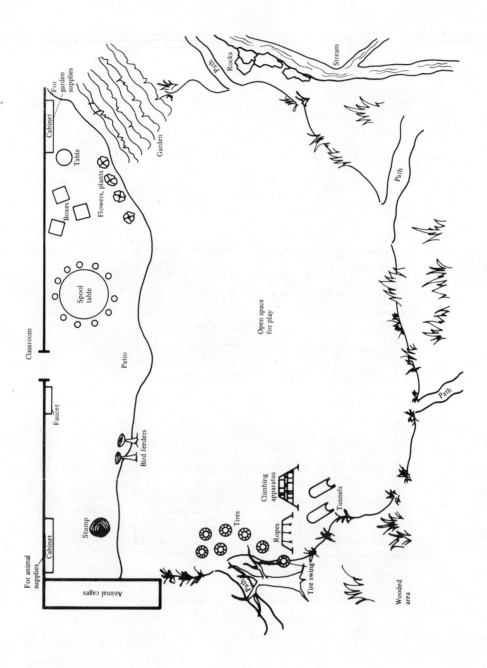

APPENDIX A

RESOURCE MATERIALS—OPEN LEARNING

Books, Booklets, and Pamphlets

Advisory Centre for Education. *Where*. Advisory Centre for Education, 57 Russell Street, Cambridge, England.

Allen, Gwen, et al. *Scientific Interests in the Primary School*. National Froebel Foundation, 2 Manchester Square, London W.1., 1966.

Barth, Roland S. *Open Education and the American School*. New York: Agathen Press, Inc., 1972.

Blitz, Barbara. *The Open Classroom*: *Making It Work*. Boston, Mass.: Allyn and Bacon, Inc., 1973.

Blackie, John. *Inside the Primary School*. London: Her Majesty's Stationery Office, 1967 (paper). Available in the U.S. through Sales Section, British Information Services, 845 Third Avenue, New York, N.Y. 10022.

Boyle, D.G., *A Student's Guide to Piaget*. Oxford: Aterganion Press,1969.

Brearley, M., et al. *Fundamentals in the First School*. Oxford, Eng.: Basil Blackwell & Mott Ltd., 1970.

Brearley, Molley, ed. *The Teaching of Young Children*: *Some Applications of Piaget's Learning Theory*. New York: Schocken Books, Inc., 1970.

Brown, Mary, and Norman Precious. *The Integrated Day in the Primary School*. London: Ward Lock Educational Co., Ltd., 1968 (New York: Agathon Press, Inc., 1970).

Brenner, John, and Ann Brenner. *Open Education—A Beginning*. New York: Holt, Rinehart and Winston, Inc., 1972.

Cass, Joan, and D.E.M. Gardner. *The Role of the Teacher in the Infant and Nursery School*. London: Pergamon Press, 1965.

Cazden, Courtney B. *Infant School*. Education Development Center, 55 Chapel Street, Newton, Mass. 1969.

Center for Curriculum Renewal and Educational Development Overseas. *Children at School*: *Primary Education in Britain Today*. London: Heineman Educational Books, Ltd., 1969.

Chittenden, Edward A., and others. *Analysis of an Approach to Open Education*. Princeton, N.J.: Educational Testing Service, 1970.

Clegg, Sir Alec. *Revolution in the British Primary Schools*. Washington, D.C.: NAESP, 1971.

Consultative Committee on the Primary School. *The Hadow Report*: *A Report of the Consultative Committee on the Primary School*. London: Her Majesty's Stationery Office, 1931 (reprinted 1962). Available in the U.S. through Sales Section, British Information Services, 845 Third Avenue, New York, N.Y. 10022.

Cooper, Gertrude E. *The Place of Play in an Infant and Junior School*. London: National Froebel Foundation, 1966. Available from National Froebel Foundation, 2 Manchester Square, London W.1.

Copeland, Richard W. *How Children Learn Mathematics*, 2nd ed. New York: Macmillan Publishing Co., Inc., 1974.

Copeland, Richard W. *Diagnostic and Learning Activities for Children*. New York: Macmillan Publishing Co., Inc., 1974.

Dean, Joan. *Informal Schools in Britain Today*: *Recording Children's Progress*. New York: Citation Press, 1972.

Dimondstein, Geraldine, *Exploring the Arts with Children*. New York: Macmillan Publishing Co., Inc., 1974.

Dunn, Rita, and Kenneth Dunn. *Practical Approaches to Individualizing Instruction*: *Contracts and Other Effective Teaching Strategies*. West Nyack, N.Y.: Parker Publishing Co., Inc., 1972.

Early Childhood Education Study. *Occasional Papers*. Early Childhood Education Study, 55 Chapel Street, Newton Mass. 02160.

Early Education Environment. Special Report. *Grade Teacher*, 88: 36–41 (December 1970).

EKNE. *Multi-Age Grouping*: *Enriching the Learning Environment*. Washington, D.C.: EKNE, 1968.

Evans, Ellis D. *Contemporary Influences in Early Childhood Education*. New York: Holt, Rinehart and Winston, Inc., 1971.

Featherstone, Joseph. *Schools Where Children Learn*. New York: Liveright Publishing Corp., 1971.

Frazier, Alexander. *Open Schools for Children*. Association for Supervision and Curriculum Development, 1972.

Franklin, Marian, Pope, ed. *Classroom Centers and Stations in America and Britain*. New York: MSS Information Corporation, 655 Madison Avenue, New York, N.Y. 1973.

Furth, Hans G. *Piaget for Teachers*. Englewood Cliffs, N.J.: Prentice-Hall, Inc., 1970.

Goddell, Carol. *The Changing Classroom*. New York: Balantine Books, Inc., 1973.

Glasser, William. *The Effect of School Failure on the Life of a Child*. Washington, D.C.: NAESP, 1971.

Hassett and Weisberg. *Open Education*: *Alternatives Within Our Tradition*. Englewood Cliffs, N.J.: Prentice-Hall, Inc., 1972.

Hertzberg, Alvin, and Edward F. Stone. *Schools Are for Children*. New York: Schocken Books, Inc., 1971.

Hess, Robert D., and Doreen J. Croft. *Teachers of Young Children*. Boston: Houghton Mifflin Company, 1972.

Hildebrand, Verna. *Introduction to Early Childhood Education*. New York: Macmillan Publishing Co., Inc., 1971.

Holt, John. *Freedom and Beyond*. New York: E.P. Dutton and Co., Inc., 1972.

Holt, John. *How Children Fail*. New York: Pitman Publishing Corp., 1964. @ $4.50. Also available in paperback @ $1.75 from Dell Publishing Co.

Holt, John. *How Children Learn*. New York: Pitman Publishing Corp., 1967.

Holt, John. *The Underachieving School*. New York: Pitman Publishing Corp., 1969.

Holt, John. *What Do I Do Monday*? New York: E.P. Dutton & Co., Inc., 1970.

Howard, Leo M. *The Developmental Classroom*. Boston: Office of Program Development (unpublished mimeograph), 1968. Single copies available from the author c/o Assistant Director, W.L.P. Boardman School, 29 Hazelwood Street, Roxbury, Mass.

Howes, Virgil M. *Informal Teaching in the Open Classroom*. New York: Macmillan Publishing Co., Inc., 1974.

Howson, Geoffrey. *Children at School*: *Primary Education in Britain Today*. New York: Teachers College Press, 1969.

Hymes, James L., Jr. *Teaching the Child Under Six*, 2nd ed. Columbus, Ohio: Charles E. Merrill Publishers, 1974.

Isaacs, Nathan. *Piaget*: *Some Answers to Teacher's Questions*. National Froebel Foundation, 2 Manchester Square, London W.1., 1965, @ 3/0d.

Isaacs, Susan. *The Children We Teach*: *Seven to Eleven Years*. University of London Press Ltd., 1932 (reprinted 1967). @ 7/6d.

James, Charity. *Young Lives at Stake*: *A Reappraisal of Secondary Schools*. London: Collins, 1968.

Kahl, David H., and Barbara T. Gast. *Learning Centers in the Open Classroom*. Encino, Calif.: International Center for Educational Development, 1974.

Kinney, Gloria, ed. *The Ideal School*. Wilmette, Ill.: Kagg Press, 1969.

Kohl, Herbert R. *The Open Classroom*. New York: The New York Review, 1972.

Kohl, Herbert R. *The Open Classroom*: *A Practical Guide to a New Way of Teaching*. New York: Vintage Books, 1969.

Leeper, Sarah Hammond. *Good Schools for Young Children*: *A Guide for Working With Three-, Four-, and Five-Year-Old Children*. Macmillan Publishing Co., Inc., 1974.

Mann, Beatrice F. *Learning Through Creative Work* (*The Under 8's in School*). National Froebel Foundation, 2 Manchester Square, London W.1., 1961 (revised 1966).

Margolin, Edythe. *Sociocultural Elements in Early Childhood Education*. New York: Macmillan Publishing Co., Inc., 1974.

Marshall, Sybil. *Adventure in Creative Education*. London: Pergamon Press, Ltd., 1968. Available in the United States through offices at 22-01 21st Street, Long Island City, N.Y. 11101.

Mayer, Robert. *Preparing Instructional Objectives*. Belmont, Calif.: Fearon Publishers, 1962. A book for teachers and student teachers—for anyone interested in transmitting skills and knowledge.

Milgram, Joel I., and Dorothy June Sciarra. *Childhood Revisited*. New York: Macmillan Publishing Co., Inc., 1974.

Mills, Belen Collantes. *Understanding the Young Child and His Curriculum*. New York: Macmillan Publishing Co., Inc., 1972.

✓Murrow, Casey, and Liza Murrow. *Children Come First*. New York: American Heritage Press, 1971.

Myers, R.E. "Comparison of the Perceptions of Elementary School Children in Open Area and Self Contained Classrooms in British Colombia: Ideal Teacher Checklist." *J. Res. and Develop. Education*, 4 (Spring 1971), 100-106.

National Elementary Principal: *Perspectives in Open Education*. Washington, D.C.: NAESP, November 1972.

Nyquist, Ewald B., and Gene R. Hawes, eds. *Open Education. A Sourcebook for Parents and Teachers*. New York: Bantam Books, Inc., 1972.

Open Education—ESEA Title I, Theresa, Theater, and Terrariums. Albany: University of New York. State Education Department, Division of Education for the Disadvantaged.

Perrone, Vito. *Open Education*: *Promise and Problems*. Bloomington, Ind.: Phi Delta Kappa Education Foundation, 1972.

Peters, R.S., ed. *Prespectives on Plowden*. London: Routledge and Kegan Paul Ltd., and New York: Humanities Press, 1969.

Pines, Maya. *Revolution in Learning*: *The Years from Birth to Six*. New York: Harper & Row, Publishers, Inc., 1967.

Plowden, Lady Bridget, et al. *Children and Their Primary Schools*: *A Report of the Central Advisory Council for Education*. London: Her Majesty's Stationery Office, 1966. Available through Sales Section, British Information Services, 845 Third Avenue, New York, N.Y. 10022 (Vol. I @ 5.00; Vol. II @ 6.50.)

Praker, G.F. *The Plowden Children 4 Years Later*. London: National Foundation for Educational Research in England and Wales, 1971.

Program Reference Service. Open Door. New York: Center for Urban Education, 1971.

Rapport, V., assoc. ed. *Learning Centers*: *Children on Their Own.* Washington D.C.: Association for Childhood Education International, 1970.

Rathbone, Charles H., ed. *Open Education*: *The Informal Classroom.* New York: Citation Press, 1971.

Ridgway, Lorna, and Irene Lawton. *Family Grouping in the Primary School.* New York: Ballantine Books, Inc., 1973.

Rogers, Vincent R. *Teaching in the British Primary School.* New York: Macmillan Publishing Co., Inc., 1970.

Rosenthal, Robert, and Lenore Jacobson. *Pygmalion in the Classroom.* New York: Holt, Rinehart and Winston, Inc., 1968. Teacher Expectation and Pupils' Intellectual Development.

Silberman, Charles E. *Crisis in the Classroom*: *The Remaking of American Education.* New York: Random House, Inc., 1970.

Silberman, Charles E. *The Open Classroom Reader.* New York: Vintage Books, 1973.

Spodek, Bernard. *Early Childhood Education.* Englewood Cliffs, N.J.: Prentice-Hall, Inc., 1973.

Spodek, Bernard. *Teaching in the Early Years.* Englewood Cliffs, N.J.: Prentice-Hall, Inc., 1972.

Stephens, Lillian S. *The Teacher's Guide to Open Education.* Holt, Rinehart and Winston, Inc., 1974.

Taylor, Joy. *Organizing and Integrating the Infant Day.* London: George Allen and Unwin, Ltd., 1971.

Taylor, Katherine W. *Parents and Children Learn Together.* New York: Teachers College Press, 1967.

Thatcher, David A. *Teaching, Loving and Self-Directed Learning.* Pacific Palisades, Calif.: Goodyear Publishing Co., Inc., 1973.

The Education Digest. Washington, D.C.: American Association of School Administrators, 1971, chap. 3, pp. 19-25.

Thomas, George, and Joseph Crescimbeni. *Individualizing Instruction in the Elementary School.* New York: Random House, Inc., 1967.

University of London Institute of Education. *First Years in School.* London: George G. Harrap & Co. Ltd., 1963. (Reprinted 1967.) @ 12/6d.

Voight, Ralph Claude. *Invitation to Learning*: *The Learning Center Handbook.* Washington, D.C.: Acropolis Books, Ltd., 1971.

Walters, Elsa H. *Activity and Experience in the Infant School.* National Froebel Foundation, 2 Manchester Square, London W.1.

Walton, Jack. *The Integrated Day in Theory and Practice.* London: Wardlock Educational Co., Ltd., 1971.

Weber, Lillian. *The English Infant School and Informal Education.* Englewood Cliffs, N.J.: Prentice-Hall, Inc., 1971.

Wurman, Richard Saul, ed. *Yellow Pages of Learning Resources.* Cambridge, Mass.: MIT Press, 1972.

Yeomans, Edward. *Preparing Teachers for the Integrated Day*. Boston: National Association of Independent Schools, 1972.

Articles

"Americanizing the Open School." *Nation's Schools* (Spring 1972), 45–48.

Anderson, D.C. "Open Plan Schools: Time for a Peek at Lady Godiva." *Ed. Can.*, **10** (June 1970), 2–6.

Andreae, Jenny C. "Developing Open Classrooms in New Rochelle." *Open Education*, edited by Ewald B. Nyquist and Gene R. Hawes. New York: Bantam Books, Inc., 1972.

Barth, Roland S. "Open Education: Assumptions About Learning and Knowledge." *Educational Philosophy and Theory*. Oxford: Pergamon Press, October 1969.

Barth, Roland S., and Charles Rathbone. "Informal Education—the Open School: A Way of Thinking About Children, Learning, Knowledge." *Center Forum*, July 1969. Also appeared in *Open Education*, edited by Ewald B. Nyquist and Gene R. Hawes. New York: Bantam Books, Inc., 1972.

Berstein, Basil. "The Open School." *Where*. (Supplement #12). Advisory Center for Education, 57 Russell Street, Cambridge, England, 1967.

Berson, M.P. "Inside the Open Classroom." *American Education*, **7** (May 1971), 11–15.

Berson, Minnie P. "Inside the Open Classroom." *Childhood Education*, **7** (May 1966), 11–15.

Burnham, Brian. "Open Education: Some Research Answers to Basic Questions." *Orbit* (December 1971), 20–30.

Busselle, Samuel. "Training Teachers to Work in Open Space." *National Elementary Principal*, **52**:1 (September 1972), 87–90.

"Can British School Reforms Work Here?" *Nation's Schools*, **87** (May 1971), 47–51.

"Can British School Reforms Work Here?" *Educational Digest*; **37** (September 1971), 5–8.

Carlson, Robert A. "Evaluating an Open School." *National Elementary Principal*, **52**:5 (February 1973), 96–98.

Chittenden, Edward A., and Anne M. Bussis. "Open Education: Research and Assessment Strategies." *Open Education*, edited by Ewald B. Nyquist and Gene R. Hawes. New York: Bantam Books, Inc., 1972.

Cohen, David K. "Children and Their Primary Schools: Volume II." *Harvard Educational Review*, **38**:2 (Spring 1968). Single copies available @ $1.00 from H.E.R. Editorial Offices, Longfellow Hall, Cambridge, Mass.

Day, Barbara D. *Assuring Every Child the Right to Read*. "The British Infant Schools, Where Reading Is Fun." North Carolina Council of the International Reading Association (January 1973), 61–69.

Day, Barbara D. *Contemporary Trends in Early Childhood Education*. "Open Education in Great Britain and in North Carolina." SACUS (Spring 1972), 19–72.

Day, Barbara D. "Open Education Comes of Age." *North Carolina Education*, **2** (September 1971), 10–17.

"Does School + Joy = Learning?." *Newsweek*, **77** (May 3, 1971), 60–68.

Dopyera, John. "What Is Open About Open Education? Some Strategies and Results." New York: Syracuse University, January 1972, 25 pp.

Dunbar, H.S. "No Doors Slam Here: Open Space Primary School at Sidney, New York." *N.Y. State Education*, **58** (November 1970), 34–35.

Ellison, Martha. "Open Education . . . Not for the Tired or the Timid." *Kentucky School Journal* (May 1972), 17–20.

Featherstone, Joseph. "Experiments in Learning." *The New Republic*, **159**:24 (December 14, 1968).

Featherstone, Joseph. "A New Kind of Schooling." *The New Republic*, **158**:9 (March 2, 1968).

Featherstone, Joseph. "The Primary School Revolution in Britain." *The New Republic*, 1244–19th Street, N.W., Washington, D.C. 20036, 1967.

Featherstone, Joseph. "Report Analysis: Children and Their Primary Schools." *Harvard Educational Review*, **38**:2 (Spring 1968). Single reprints available @ $1.00 from H.E.R. Editorial Offices, Longfellow Hall, Cambridge, Mass. 02138.

Featherstone, Joseph. "Schools for Children: What's Happening in British Classrooms?" *The New Republic*, **157** (August 19, 1967), 17–21.

Featherstone, Joseph. "Schools for Learning." *The New Republic*, **159**:25–26 (December 21, 1968).

Featherstone, Joseph. "Relevance to the American Setting." *Open Education*, edited by Ewald B. Nyquist and Gene R. Hawes. New York: Bantam Books, Inc., 1972.

Featherstone, Joseph. "Tempering a Fad," *An Introduction*, chap. 7, 1971.

Flurry, Ruth C. "How Else?" *Young Children*, **25**:3 (January 1970). Washington, D.C.: National Association for the Education of Young Children.

Flurry, Ruth C. "Open Education: What Is It?" *Open Education*, edited by Ewald B. Nyquist and Gene R. Hawes. New York: Bantam Books, Inc., 1972.

Gross, Beatrice, and Ronald Gross. "A Little Bit of Chaos." *Saturday Review*, May 16, 1970. Also appeared in *Open Education* edited by Ewald B. Nyquist and Gene R. Hawes. New York: Bantam Books, Inc., 1972.

Hapgood, Marilyn. "The Open Classroom: Protect It from Its Friends." *Saturday Review* (Spring 1971), 66–68.

Hawkins, David. "Messing About in Science." *Science and Children*, **3**:3 (Summer and Fall 1965). Also available in single copies as Occasional Paper #2 from Early Childhood Education Study, Newton, Mass.

Hawkins, David. "Childhood and the Education of Intellectuals." *Harvard Educational Review*, **36**:4 (Fall 1966). Reprints available @ $.35 from H.E.R., Editorial Offices: Longfellow Hall, Cambridge, Mass.

Hull, W.P. "Leicestershire Revisited." *Occasional Paper #1*, 1969. Single copies available free from Early Childhood Education Study, 55 Chapel Street, Newton, Mass. 02160.

Hymes, James. "Childhood in Early Education." *Theory into Practice*, **12**: 2 (April 1973).

Killough, K. "Open Plan School." *Instructor*, **80** (August 1970), 75–76.

Knox, Gerald M. "How to Make Schools Fit for Children." *Better Homes and Gardens*, November 1972.

Kohn, Sherwood D. "Vito Perrone and North Dakota's Quiet Revolution." *National Elementary Principal*, **52**:3 (November 1972), 49–57.

MacBeth, Edwin W. "When the Walls Come Tumbling Down." *School Management*, **15** (August 1971), 8–11.

Marshall, Hermine H. "Criteria for an Open Classroom." *Young Children*, **28**:1 (October 1972), 13–19.

McNally, L., and G. Gleming. "Quest for Alternative." *Ed. Lead*, **28** (February 1971), 490–493.

Nasca, Donald. "Open Education: Is It For You?" *Instructor*, **83**:2 (October 1973), 93–98.

Nyquist, Ewald B. "Open Education: Its Philosophy, Historical Perspectives and Implications." *Open Education*, edited by Ewald B. Nyquist and Gene R. Hawes. New York: Bantam Books, Inc., 1972.

Nyquist, Ewald B. "The Concept of Open Education." *Science Teacher* (September 1971), 25–28.

"One Room Schoolhouse 1972 Style; Middle Island School District, New York." School Mgt., **15** (April 1971), 17–20.

Opdyke, Jeanne B. "Without Walls and Doors." *Ind. School Bullentin* **29** (December 1969), 34–36.

"Open Education: Can British School Reforms Work Here?" *Nation's Schools*, **87**:5 (May 1971).

"Open Education: An Expert Talks About Implications for Reform." *Nation's Schools*, **87** (May 1971), 56–59.

"Open Plan." *School Mgt.*, **15** (August 1971), 8–17.

Pasnik, M. "Factory Building to Modern School in Six Months." *School Mgt.*, **15** (July 1971), 12–14.

Pearce, Lucia. "Exploration–Innovation: The New Learning Environment." *The Science Teacher*, **36**:2 (February 1969).

Pilcher, Paul S. "Open Education: In Britain and the U.S.A." *Education Digest* (Fall 1972), 75–79.

"Put It All Together School: Walnut Hills School, Englewood, Colorado." *Instructor*, **80** (April 1971), 60–62.

Raggatt, Peter C.M. "Administration in British Primary Schools." *National Elementary Principal*, **52**:3 (November 1972), 25–29.

Rathbone, Charles. "Assessing the Alternatives." *Childhood Education*, **47** (February 1971), 234–238.

Richman, Vivien C. "Open Education: Notes on Implementation." *Grade Teacher* (April 1972).

Rogers, Vincent R. "Open Education." *Instructor*, **81** (August 1971), 74–76.

Rogers, Vincent R. "Open Schools on the British Model." *Educational Leadership* (February 1972). Journal of Association for Supervision and Curriculum Development, N.E.A.

Rogers, Vincent R. "Vincent Rogers Answers Your Questions on Open Education." *Instructor*, **81** (August/September 1971), 74–76.

Sartore, Richard L. "A Principal with a New Outlook Is Needed in the Open School." *The Clearing House*, **42**:3 (November 1972), 131–134.

Schubert, Delwyn. "Individulized Self-Directed Correction." *Elementary English*, **50** (March 1973), 441–443.

Silberman, Charles E. "It Can Happen Here," *Crisis in the Classroom*. New York: Random House, Inc., 1970.

Silberman, Charles E. "The Case of the New English Primary School," *Crisis in the Classroom*. New York: Random House, Inc., 1970.

Silberman, Charles E. "Murder in the Schoolroom." *The Atlantic* (July 1970).

Spodek, Bernard. "Alternatives to Traditional Education." *Peabody Journal of Education*, **158** (January 1971), 140–146.

Spodek, Bernard. "Extending Open Education in the United States." *Open Education*, edited by Ewald B. Nyquist and Gene R. Hawes. New York: Bantam Books, Inc., 1972.

Staple, I.E. "Open-Space Plan in Education." *Educational Leadership*, **28** (February 1971), 458–463.

Stewart, James W., and Jack Shank. "Student-Teacher Contracting: A Vehicle for Individualizing Instruction." *Audiovisual Instruction*, **18** (January 1973), 31–34.

Tag, H.G. "Integrated Day: British Style." *Peabody J. Education*, **48** (July 1971), 325–330.

Thomas, J.E. "Pod Units in an Open Elementary School." *School and Community*, **57** (April 1971), 12–13.

Tobier, Arthur J. "The Open Classroom: Humanizing the Coldness of Public Places." *The Center Forum*, 3:6 (May 15, 1969). Center for Urban Education, 105 Madison Avenue, New York, N.Y.

"Trying the Momentous Alternative of Open Education—Introduction to *Open Education*, edited by Ewald B. Nyquist and Gene R. Hawes. New York: Bantam Books, Inc., 1972.

Ulin, Donald S. "What I Learned from the British Schools." *Grade Teacher*, **86**:6 (February 1969). Copies of entire issue @ $1.00 from 23 Leroy Avenue, Darien, Conn.

Ury, E.M. "Early Childhood Education Programs." *Education*, **91** (November 1970), 107–109.

Wing, R.C., and P.H. Mack. "Wide Open for Learning: Project SOLVE, N.H." *American Education*, **6** (November 1970), 13–15.

Walberg, Herbert J., and Susan Christie Thomas. "Open Education: An Operational Definition and Validation in Great Britain and U.S." *American Educational Research Journal* (Spring 1972), 197–204.

Weber, Lillian. "Development in Open Corridor Organization." *National Elementary Principal*, **52**:3 (November 1972), 58–67.

Wilson, F.S.; T. Stuckey; and R. Langevin. "Are Pupils in the Open Plan School Different?" *Journal of Educational Research*, **66**:3 (November 1972), 115–118.

Wilson, Robert M., and Linda B. Gambrell. "Contracting—One Way to Individualize." *Elementary English*, **50** (March 1973), 427–429.

Films

Battling Brook Primary School (*Four Days in September*): *An Overview Plus Several Vignettes*. Education Development Center, 55 Chapel Street, Newton, Mass. 02160.

Children Are People. Agathon Press, Inc., 150 Fifth Avenue, New York, N.Y. 10011.

Children Are People. Polymorph Films, Inc., Newbury St., Boston, Mass. 02115.

Discovery and Experience (Series includes 10 films): *Learning by Doing, Math Is a Master, Our Own Music, Learning by Design, Finding Out, Movement in Time and Space, The Changeover, City Infants, The Growing Mind, How Children Think*. Produced by British Broadcasting Corporation. Available in the U.S.A. from Time–Life Films. 1271 Sixth Avenue, New York, N.Y. 10020.

I Am Here Today. Educational Development Center, Inc., 55 Chapel Street, Newton, Mass. 02160.

I Do and I Understand. Educational Foundation for Visual Aids, 33 Queen Anne Street, London, WIM OAL (England).

Infants School. Education Development Center, Inc., 55 Chapel Street, Newton, Mass. 02160.

Living and Learning in the Open Classroom. International Center for Educational Development, 16161. Ventura Blvd., Encino, Calif. 91316.

Maths Alive. Educational Foundations for Visual Aids, 33 Queen Anne Street, London WIM OAL (England).

Medbourne Primary School—Four Days in May. Education Development Center, 55 Chapel Street, Newton, Mass. 02160.

Open Classroom. Sherwin Rubin, 4532 Newton St., Torrance, Calif. 90505.

Primary Adventure. Inner London Education Authority. The County Hall, London, SE1, England.

Primary Education in England: *The English Infant School*. I/D/E/A, Information Division, P.O. Box 446, Melbourne, Florida 32901.

Room to Learn. Association Films, Inc., Madison Avenue, New York, N.Y. 10022.

School Without Failure. Media Five, Film Distributors, 1011 North Cole Avenue, Hollywood, Calif. 90038.

The British Infant School—Southern Style. Promethean Films South, P.O. Box 1489, Auburn, Ala. 36830.

The Informal Classroom. Educational Coordinates, 4325. Pastoria Avenue, Sunnyvale, Calif. 94086.

Westfield Infant School: *Two Days in May.* Education Development Center, 55 Chapel Street, Newton, Mass. 02160.

What Did You Learn at School Today? Leichestershire Country Library, Clarence Street, Leichestershire LE13RW, England.

APPENDIX B

CHECKLIST OF MATERIALS FOR LEARNING CENTERS

Language Arts Center

1. Reading games—commerical and teacher-made
2. Reading skills kits
3. Flannel boards and cutouts
4. Large alphabet blocks
5. Puzzles
6. Sequence cards
7. Chalkboards
8. Magnetic board
9. Pictures and objects for classifying
10. Magazines and catalogs
11. Writing paper of different sizes and shapes
12. Pencils, colored marking pens, crayons
13. Poems and story starters
14. Blank booklets
15. Dictionaries
16. Book jackets
17. Word boxes
18. Typewriter
19. Feel box

20. Magic slates
21. Word cards
22. Filmstrips, tapes, records related to reading
23. Manipulative devices for visual discrimination and motor coordination

Reading Center

1. Large area rug or carpet
2. Pillows or floor cushions
3. Rocking chairs
4. Easy chairs and couch
5. Assortments of books (library books, basal readers, etc.)
6. Magazines and catalogs
7. Encyclopedias
8. Child-made books
9. Shelves (low)
10. Flannel board and story characters
11. Puppets
12. Viewmasters and slides of stories
13. Filmstrips of stories
14. Tape recorder for children to tape themselves reading
15. Record player and records with corresponding book

Block Center

1. Set of solid wooden blocks
   Unit blocks
   Double unit blocks
   Quadruple unit blocks
   Ramps
   Curves (elliptical and circular)
   Y shapes
   Triangles
   Cylinders
2. Set of hollow-ply blocks (varying in size)
3. Riding wheel toys (tractor and trailer, derrick truck, open van truck)
4. Small vehicles (airplane, helicopter, dump truck, steamroller, train, firetruck)
5. Block bin
6. Block cart
7. Rubber zoo and farm animals
8. Rubber people (farmer, policeman, etc.)
9. Traffic signs
10. Steering wheel

Math Center

1. Counters (blocks, beads, sticks, straws, buttons, clothespins, bottle caps, etc.)
2. Scales and objects to weigh
3. Rulers, yardstick, tape measure
4. Thermometers
5. Clocks
6. Measuring devices (spoons, cup, quart, etc.)
7. Math books
8. Commercial and teacher–made games
   (see directions for making)
9. Bead or counting frame
10. Cuisenaire rods
11. Number lines
12. Balances
13. Play money
14. Geoboards
15. Flannel board and cutouts
16. Pegs and pegboards
17. Dominoes
18. Problem or activity cards
19. Attribute blocks
20. Acetate folders for worksheets
21. Place value charts

Woodworking Center

1. Workbench
2. Sawhorse
3. Storage shelves
4. Hand drill with several bits
5. 4″ "C" clamps
6. File, cabinet, half round 8 in.
7. File card for cleaning file
8. Hammer, claw—7 oz.
9. Pliers, combination, 6 in.
10. Saw, hand crosscut, 16 and 11 pt.
11. Saw, coping (for cutting curves)
12. Screwdriver, 4 in.
13. Vise for workbench
14. Backsaw
15. T-square
16. Miter box
17. Paint scraper
18. Brush

19. Broom, dustpan
20. Nails (variety)
21. Hooks and screws
22. Paint
23. Trash can with lid
24. Paint stain
25. Paint brushes
26. Wood scraps
27. Rulers, yardstick
28. Rags
29. Scissors
30. Glue (Elmer's)

Science Center

1. Large aquarium
2. Bird-feeding station
3. Magnifying glass (hand, tripod)
4. Cages for insects
5. Cages for live animals
6. Different kinds of soil
7. Magnets (bar, U, horseshoe)
8. Science kits
9. Prism
10. Seeds to plant and classify
11. Watering cans
12. Objects that float and do not float
13. Terrarium
14. Objects to smell, taste, hear, touch, see
15. Thermometers—outdoor and indoor
16. Things to take apart and put together
17. Pulleys, levers, etc.
18. Simple machines
19. Electrical equipment
20. Compass
21. Shapes
22. Things to classify
23. Flower boxes
24. Rock and shell collections

Social Studies Center

1. Maps (city, neighborhood, state, U.S., world)

2. Globe (primary)
3. Pictures and study prints
4. Magazines and catalogs
5. Question and problem cards
6. Teacher–made activity cards
7. Social studies books
8. Encyclopedias
9. Filmstrips relating to social studies
10. Class books about social studies topics
11. Charts of information
12. Models of workers, stores, Indians, vehicles, radios, etc.
13. Equipment such as telephone to take apart
14. Scrapbooks
15. Materials to make a diorama, peep box, models, etc.

Creative Dramatics

1. Puppets
2. Puppet theater
3. Brooms, mop, dustpan
4. Brushes
5. Clothes rack
6. Dish pan
7. Child–size wooden sink, stove, refrigerator, cupboard
8. Small table, chairs
9. Small rug
10. Shelves
11. Chest for dress–up clothes, shoes, hats
12. Dolls
13. Doll clothes
14. Doll bed
15. Cooking utensils
16. Sponges, cloths
17. Doll carriage
18. Dishes, silverware
19. Mirror
20. Rocking chair
21. Curtains for window
22. Artificial fruits, vegetables
23. Telephone
24. Ironing board, iron
25. Pails
26. Jewelry, shoes, handbags, hats, coats, dresses for play, props for playing doctor, beauty parlor, etc.

Music Center

1. Rhythm instruments
2. Small boxes
3. Dowel sticks
4. Record player
5. Records
6. Earphones
7. Autoharp
8. Music books and charts of songs to play
9. Glasses of water and spoons
10. Manuscript paper for children to write songs
11. Scarves for dancing
12. Materials for children to make their own instruments (boxes, paper plates, bottle caps, pebbles, stones, beans, cans, etc.)

Art Center

1. Materials for weaving, stitchery
2. Box of materials for collages
3. Bags
4. Socks
5. Art prints and art objects
6. Books of crafts, artists, pictures of paintings
7. Box of paper scraps and material scraps
8. Magazines and catalogs
9. Wallpaper samples
10. Aprons, old shirts, or smocks
11. Orange juice cans
12. Corn starch, laundry starch
13. Flour, salt (for play dough)
14. Drying rack
15. Florist wire
16. Electrical wire
17. Colored toothpicks
18. Plastic garbage can with lid for clay (pottery)
19. Cake tins for modeling clay
20. Containers with lids for mixed paints
21. Clay boards (9″ × 12″ hot mats), cafeteria trays
22. Paper clips, brads, staples, pins
23. Food coloring
24. Buttons, different shapes of macaroni, nuts, caps, etc.
25. Wood scraps
26. Scissors
27. Paint (Tempera)

28. Paste
29. Glue (Elmer's)
30. Tape
31. Rubber cement
32. Stapler
33. Magic Markers
34. Pencils (lead, colored)
35. Finger paint
36. Rulers
37. Plaster of Paris
38. Colored chalk and pastels
39. Easel
40. Pipe cleaners
41. Looms
42. Yarn
43. Charcoal
44. Water colors
45. Modeling clay
46. Pottery clay
47. Paint brushes
48. Crayons
49. Construction paper
50. Finger-painting paper
51. Art tissue
52. Crepe paper
53. Corrugated cardboard
54. Fadeless paper
55. Instant papier-maché

Quiet Area

1. Rugs
2. Pillows
3. Rocking chair
4. Separated by a screen or drape of material
5. This should be a quiet place where a child may go to be alone to think or do what he wishes. It should be a comfortable and relaxing area but include no specific materials. Children may bring their own materials to this center.

Outdoor Centers

1. Sand and water play table with top
2. Aluminum sand utensils
3. Sailboat

 4. Jungle gym
 5. Sandbox
 6. Tire swings
 7. Platforms
 8. Large sewer pipes (set in cement)
 9. Tree trunks
10. Low turning bars
11. Low horizontal ladders
12. Safety climbing tree
13. Low climbing ropes
14. Wading pool
15. Walking boards (cleated and various lengths—4' to 6' and 8" to 12" wide)
16. Sawhorses (various heights)
17. Ladders (cleats at each end, 3" to 5')
18. Wooden steps
19. Heavy wooden benches
20. Low balance beams
21. Bales of straw
22. Tires—tractor, automobile, bicycle
23. Balls (various sizes—8" to 24")
24. Beanbags
25. Jump ropes—long and individual
26. Riding toys (wagons, tricycles, wheelbarrows, etc.)
27. Sand toys
28. Tools for gardening—shovels, rakes, hoes, etc.
29. Building blocks
30. Tools for woodwork
31. Water hose
32. Large packing boxes

APPENDIX C

SUGGESTED REFERENCES ON PRODUCTION OF TEACHER—MADE MATERIALS

Allen, Roach V. *Language Experiences in Early Childhood*. Chicago: Encyclopaedia Britannica Press, 1966.

Espich, James E., and Bill Williams. *Developing Programmed Instructional Materials*. Belmont, Calif. Fearon Publishers/Lear Siegler, Inc.

Glazier, Raye. *How to Design Educational Games*. Cambridge: ABT Associates, Inc., 1971.

Hayett, William. *Display and Exhibit Handbook*. New York: Reinhold Publishing Corp., 1967.

Kemp, Jerrold E. *Planning and Producing Audiovisual Materials*, 2nd ed. Scranton, Penn.: Chandler Publishing Co.

Matterson, E.M. *Play and Playthings for the Pre-School Child*. Baltimore: Penguin Books, Inc., 1970.

Minor, Ed. *Preparing Visual Instructional Materials*. New York: McGraw-Hill Book Company, 1962.

Norlan, John E. *Preparation of Inexpensive Teaching Materials*. San Francisco: Chandler Publishing Co., 1963.

Petty Walter R., and Mary E. Bowen. *Slithery Snakes and Other Aids to Children's Writing*. New York: Appleton-Century-Crofts, 1967.

Smith, Hayden R., and Thomas S. Nagel. *Instructional Media in the Learning Process*, Columbus, Ohio: Charles E. Merrill Publishing Co., 1972.

Smith, James A. Boston: Allyn and Bacon, Inc. Series in Creative Teaching.
  Creative Teaching of the Language Arts
  Creative Teaching of Reading and Literature
  Creative Teaching of the Creative Arts
  Creative Teaching of the Social Studies
  Creative Teaching of Mathematics
  Creative Teaching of Science in the Elementary School
Stone Mountain Education Projects Inc., *Preschool Equipment*. Conway, Mass.,
  1972.
Turner, Ethel M. *Teaching Aids for Elementary Mathematics*. New York:
  Holt, Rinehart and Winston, Inc., 1966.
Voight, Ralph Claude. *Invitation to Learning—The Learning Center Handbook*.
  Washington, D.C.: Acropolis Books, Ltd., 1971.

APPENDIX D

EARLY CHILDHOOD COMMERCIAL SUPPLIERS

1. ABC School Supply, Inc.
   437 Armour Cir. N.E.
   P.O. Box 13084
   Atlanta, Ga. 30324

2. American Guidance Service, Inc.
   Publisher's Building
   Circle Pines, Minn. 55014

3. Bender School Supply
   P.O. Box 128
   Pollocksville, N.C. 28573

4. Bowmar
   622 Rodier Drive
   Glendale, Calif. 91201

5. Carolina School Supply
   2619 West Boulevard
   P.O. Box 2185
   Charlotte, N.C. 28201

6. Childcraft Educational Corp.
   964 Third Avenue
   New York, N.Y. 10022

7. Community Playthings
   Rifton, N.Y. 12471

8. Constructive Playthings
   1040 East 85th St.
   Kansas City, Mo. 64131

9. Creative Playthings
   Princeton, N.J. 08540

10. Cuisenaire Company of America
    12 Church Street
    New Rochelle, N.Y. 10805

11. Developmental Learning Materials
    7440 North Natchez Ave.
    Niles, Ill. 60648

12. Eye Gate House, Inc.
146–01 Archer Ave.
Jamaica, N.Y. 11435

13. Follett Educational Corp.
1010 Washington Blvd.
Chicago, Ill. 60607

14. Ginn & Co.
717 Miami Circle
Atlanta, Ga. 30324

15. Holt, Rinehart and Winston, Inc.
383 Madison Ave.
New York, N.Y. 10017

16. Houghton Mifflin Co.
666 Miami Circle, N.E.
Atlanta, Ga., 30324

17. Imperial International Learning
Corp.
c/o Carolina School Supply
2619 West Boulevard
P.O. Box 2185
Charlotte, N.C. 28201

18. Instructional Aids, Inc.
Box 4193
Charlotte, N.C.

19. Knowledge Aid Division of
Milwaukee Journal Ed. Corp.
6633 W. Howard
Niles, Ill.

20. McGraw-Hill Book Co.
Webster Division
Sales Office
Manchester Rd.
Manchester, Mo. 63011

21. Milton Bradley Co.
Springfield, Mass. 00101

22. Morgan Bros. School Supply
44 Collier St.
Box 2059
Asheville, N.C. 28802

23. Scholastic Book Services
904 Sylvan Ave.
Englewood Cliffs, N.J. 07632

24. Science Research Associates, Inc.
259 East Erie St.
Chicago, Ill. 60611

25. Scott, Foresman and Co.
Tucker, Ga. 30084

26. Stones Southern School Supply
Co.
329 W. Hargett St.
Raleigh, N.C. 27602
or
500 E. Fourth St.
Charlotte, N.C. 28202

27. System 80
7450 Natchez Ave.
Niles, Ill. 60648

28. Walt Disney Educational Materials
Co.
800 Sonora Ave.
Glendale, Calif. 91201

INDEX